Llewellyn's
2011
Witches'
Companion

An Almanac for Everyday Living

Llewellyn's 2011 Witches' Companion

ISBN 978-0-7387-1137-9

Cover art © Tim Foley
Cover designer: Gavin Dayton Duffy/Lynne Menturweck
Designer: Joanna Willis
Art Director: Lynne Menturweck
Editor: Sharon Leah

Interior illustrations: Rik Olson: 52, 57, 59, 90, 92, 97, 178, 180, 183, 236, 239, 241, 245; Neil Brigham: 65, 70, 72, 116, 119, 187, 190, 192; Kathleen Edwards: 11, 14, 16, 103, 106, 109, 168, 171, 174; Tim Foley: 9, 20, 22, 24, 63, 77, 81, 87, 122, 124, 128, 131, 143, 156, 164, 197, 199, 201, 205; Paul Hoffman: 31, 33, 36, 133, 136, 139, 211, 214, 216, 219; Bri Hermanson: 43, 46, 48, 146, 151, 153, 225, 229, 233

Additional clip art illustrations: Llewellyn Art Department

Any Internet references contained in this work are current at publication time, but the publisher cannot guarantee that a specific location will continue to be maintained.

You can order Llewellyn annuals and books from *New Worlds*, Llewellyn's magazine catalog. To request a free copy of the catalog, call toll-free 1-877-NEW-WRLD, or visit our Web site at http://www.llewellyn.com.

Printed in the United States of America.

Llewellyn Worldwide Ltd.
2143 Wooddale Drive
Woodbury, MN 55125-2989
www.llewellyn.com

Contents

Witchy Living • 63

Day-by-Day Witchcraft

Witchcraft Essentials • 143

Practices, Rituals & Spells

Magical Transformations • 197

Everything Old Is New Again

The Lunar Calendar   •   247

September 2010 to December 2011

Community Forum

Must Pagans Do Everything Pagan?

Barbara Ardinger

Thirty-odd years ago, when I was a newbie Pagan, I constructed altars or shrines to goddesses and gods in all four directions in every room of the house, plus I put up another altar in the center. I hung art and crafts made by Pagans on my walls and set goddesses, gods, witches, and totems on every flat surface in the house. I lit a candle for healing every time I heard of someone in need, and made a serious study of astrology, the tarot, palmistry, and other methods of divination and reading at local psychic fairs. Doing everything Pagan can also mean collecting drums and rattles and rainsticks, carrying charged crystals in our pockets, and wearing Pagan jewelry. (We all know about Pagan jewelry races, of course—you put on all your jewelry, and the first person who can stagger to the finish line under the weight of the pentacles, amulets, charms, beads, Milagros, and little totem animals is the winner.)

Where does this kind of "doing everything Pagan" lead? To a cluttered house! I have a collection of witch figures that fills my bookcases and every other horizontal surface. This includes a couple dozen soft dolls on shelves above my bed, so when the Big One hits Southern California in the middle of the night, only the soft dolls will fall on me. I'm pretty sure I have over two hundred little witches. But every time I try to count them I get a different number. They move!

What this kind of doing everything Pagan leads to is clutter and dust, to tripping over gods and goddesses and books about goddesses and gods, and ending up with so much stuff we begin to wonder if the house is going to (a) tip over, (b) sink, or (c) explode. Although we Pagans seem to like clutter, we need to ask ourselves if this is a sustainable—or affordable—decorating style.

Say you're not a newbie anymore, and you don't buy out the whole *Sacred Source* catalog every time it arrives. Say you don't haunt gifts shops in September (as I do), looking for new little witches. Say you would like to have space in your living room for more than one visitor at a time. As a new year begins, perhaps it's time to do some housecleaning. Is it time to live more simply? Time to recycle and regift, to donate and discard? Can we be Pagans and not cling to all the

Pagan tchotchkes? Can we spread our Pagan affluence around the community?

Consider Mother Earth. Yes, her lands and oceans are filled with abundance beyond abundance—minerals, flowers, trees, cacti, animals, birds, fish, and even abundant weather. But with the planet about to tip over (metaphorically speaking) because of overpopulation and overcrowding, let's not make it worse. Let's not do everything Pagan. Let's aim for a simpler life without so much stuff in it.

"Do everything Pagan" can also be interpreted in a social sense. We can celebrate every festival of the Wheel of the Year and hold our sabbat rituals outdoors in the back yard (hoping the neighbors won't see us), in a city park (let's invite the neighbors!), or on the beach. This is, after all, how we worship the ground we walk on.

If we are well connected, we can have something Pagan to do practically every day. There are Full Moon, prosperity, and healing rituals to go to, and Pagan academic conferences, PantheaCon, workshops, book clubs, Pagan pride parades, Pagan craft fairs, Pagan drumming circles, and other wonderful gatherings of Pagans and heathens of all traditions to attend. There are online classes to take and blogs to read. We can spend our hours and days reading every single page of Witchvox. We can meet interesting people with interesting, sometimes provoking, ideas. We can do whatever we want to as long as we don't harm anyone.

It can be a wonderful life. When I was somewhat more socially inclined than I am now, I was out all the time, and I had some spectacular experiences. I've created large public rituals, attended CUUPS (Coven of Unitarian Universalist Pagans) rituals and classes, and been to Gnostic masses. I once met a man who said he speaks Paleolithic and talks to birds. I helped an artist-member of the Ordo Templi Orientis who was hanging a Tree of Life for an exhibition that she had designed for her master's project. I once went to a ritual near Pasadena; the Crips and the Bloods decided to stage a rumble at the same time. Fortunately, they were several blocks away, but as we were invoking the gods, the police helicopters started flying overhead. "Throw down your weapons." Everyone in our magic circle had the same thought at the same time—Aummmmmmm. The gangstas changed their minds, the helicopters flew away, and we went on with the ritual. I think every Pagan deserves to have memories like this to share.

But what does this level of participation in the Pagan life lead to? When do we have time to earn a living if we're at this ritual or that gathering every time the Moon moves an inch? We live in a world that demands that we pay our rent and our bills—or else. Do we want to face the "or else"?

If everything Pagan is all you talk about, have you noticed that people tend to hide under the furniture when you open your mouth?

Maybe we don't need to go out so much. Maybe we can also live a mundane life, as many of us surely do, and work at a productive job, as many of us surely do. Maybe we can pay as much attention to our Muggle friends as we do to our Pagan friends. We can also have fun with people who don't do everything Pagan.

"Do everything Pagan" can turn into an intellectual endeavor. We can haunt metaphysical bookstores and buy all the new books. Maybe actually read them. We can meditate for hours every day and the rest of the time repeat Deena Metzger's wonderful goddess chant under our breath—*Isis, Astarte, Diana, Hecate, Demeter, Kali, Inanna.* We can join intellectual chatrooms and blog our philosophical ruminations, debate whether or not the Great Parthenogenic Mother Goddess always existed or was somehow born (out of what?). We can compare the complex pantheons of Egypt and India, contrast

Greco-Roman and northern European practices, and revisit Celtic and Viking theology. We can become reconstructionists and endeavor to do rituals the way they were done in the olden days. We can post rants about what Christian missionaries stole from the cultures they found. We can even start reading books of revisionist history and learn about ancient volcanoes and what the Nummo did when they arrived in northern Africa from Sirius B (or C).

This, too, is a wonderful life. We can become really, really smart, maybe even earn a reputation for wisdom. That's because (a) if you read enough, sooner or later you'll know all the answers, and (b) if you study metaphysics long enough, you'll learn that everything can have a metaphysical interpretation. Just ask our New Age friends.

It's like being in graduate school all the time, but without the term papers and the comprehensive examinations.

But doing everything Pagan intellectually can have its pitfalls. If all you know is Pagan cosmology, or how to define "real magic," or how numerology even works with cell phone numbers, then what do you talk about if you ever meet someone who's not Pagan? What do you talk about with people standing in line at the cinema? At the DMV? During breaks at work? If everything Pagan is all you talk about, have you noticed that people tend to hide under the furniture when you open your mouth? Maybe it's time to back off and subscribe to *Newsweek* or *Time*, or to Netflix.

The highly intellectualized life tends to be an arid life. It's all air, no water, maybe some fire, but no earth. If we do everything Pagan intellectually, then we become . . . well, boring.

Finally, "doing everything Pagan" can turn into an obsessive spiritual quest. After we've read all the books, we find that reading isn't enough. Now we want a personal teacher, a coven, a tradition. Knowing the old cliché that when the student is ready the teacher will appear, we send out signals. We sign up for e-newsletters and get into listservs that sound interesting. We Google a dozen topics and click on Contact Us at the bottom of every Web site. We collar authors at book signings and quiz them on what and who they know. We go to Pagan meet-ups. And pretty soon the magical contact happens—we meet a high priestess whose words pierce our hearts, or a high priest who models the life we want to lead. We find a tradition in which we're comfortable, a set of teachings we resonate with. We take the oaths, begin our year and a day, and start piling up initiations. We do everything Pagan just as the high priest or priestess, or tradition, requires.

I can't help but wonder, if we're tied so tightly into only one tradition, are we on the road to conformity? Being a Pagan in twenty-first century America is almost, by definition, being a nonconformist. Most of us were born into standard-brand religions and we went to public schools. But as kids, we always seemed to be not quite like the other kids—we were more imaginative, we had flashes of intuition or invisible friends, we wrote music or stories or made art. We just never quite fit in. And now, having found our tradition, yes, we fit in. We've thrown off the shackles of the churches of our childhood. We ignore (or laugh at) the opinions of our parents. We've adopted what used to be called alternative lifestyles. So why do we look and talk like everyone else who's doing everything Pagan?

Some of the more extreme (and secret) traditions tell us what to eat, how to dress, who we can and cannot talk to. And how is Pagan orthodoxy different from any other kind of orthodoxy? Is Pagan fundamentalism different (except in the details) from fundamentalism in any other religion? If we're still in the mundane world enough to pay

attention to the news, then we know what fundamentalism has brought to the troubled nations of the Middle East; or what it is bringing to the Texas school board, to the creationist museums in both Kansas and Kentucky that feature dioramas showing men and dinosaurs living in the same neighborhood, or to preachers and politicians who say, "My way or the highway." What is fundamentalism bringing to the Pagan community?

How does a rebel turn into a fundamentalist? I believe it is partly by doing everything Pagan. I believe it's by jumping into the deep water and not coming up to breathe often enough. I believe it's the result of not being grounded in what most of us call the real world.

Should we do everything Pagan? I believe we should not. I believe we should do many things Pagan, but we should also aim for balance in our lives. Pagans don't live alone on the Earth. We can become a critical mass that might help the planet and humanity (and other species) survive, but we can't do that if we're just doing everything Pagan all the time. Let's live balanced Pagan lives.

Barbara Ardinger, Ph.D. (*www.barbaraardinger.com*) *is the author of* Pagan Every Day: Finding the Extraordinary in Our Ordinary Lives (*RedWheel/Weiser, 2006*), *a unique daybook of daily meditations, stories, and activities. Her earlier books include* Goddess Meditations, Finding New Goddesses (*a parody of goddess encyclopedias*), *and* Quicksilver Moon (*a realistic novel, except for the vampire*). *Her day job is freelance editing for Pagans and other people who have good ideas but limited writing skills and don't want to embarrass themselves in print. To date, she has edited more than 200 books, both fiction and nonfiction, on a wide range of topics. Barbara lives in Southern California with her Maine coon cats, Schroedinger and Heisenberg.*

Illustrator: Kathleen Edwards

Witchcraft's Christian Roots

Donald Tyson

Ask witches how they feel about Christians, and you are likely to get an angry retort. Hostility toward Christianity among the practitioners of modern witchcraft has existed for a long time, but it has risen to the boiling point in recent years. We don't have to seek far to find the root of this anger. Christian fundamentalism has enjoyed a boom of prosperity since the 1980s, and one of its primary messages is that Satan is everywhere, hiding behind every tree and under every rock. In the eyes of most devout born-again Christians, all forms of esoteric or occult practice, no matter how seemingly benign, are works of the devil.

Trying to explain to a fundamentalist that modern witches don't believe in worshipping the devil can become an exercise in futility. Nobody likes to be told that they are damned souls, who will burn in hell for eternity, but that is the response witches get when they attempt to reason with fundamentalists. Who can blame witches for throwing up their hands in disgust and turning their backs on all of Christianity? Yet in doing so, they run the risk of cutting themselves off from their own magical current, which evolved within a Christian context. Before considering this connection, let's take a quick look at how the enmity against witchcraft arose within the Christian religion.

The history of Christian persecutions against witches has its origin in the Pentateuch, that portion of the Old Testament supposed to have been written by Moses himself and that predates the birth of Jesus by several thousand years. The words of Exodus 22:18 are well known to witches. In the King James translation of the Bible, the verse reads, "Thou shalt not suffer a witch to live." This would seem to be an absolute condemnation of witchcraft, until we reflect that the word "witch" is a translation of the Hebrew word *m'khashephah*, which means "a woman who uses incantations for malicious purposes—an evil enchantress or sorceress."

The key understanding of the Hebrew term is: a woman who actively uses spells to cause harm. Clearly, this would not apply to a worshipper of the Goddess, or to a wise woman who uses herbs to heal the sick, or even to a spirit medium who communicates with the souls of the dead. Mind you, these other activities were also condemned by the law-givers of the Hebrews, but they do not fall under the term *m'khashephah* that in English came to be commonly translated as witch, and in other European countries was misinterpreted to mean the equivalent of "witch" in their various languages.

In the early Christian churches, active persecution against witches—healers, seers, makers of charms, worshippers of the Goddess—was minimal. The ire of the Church, in those early times, was directed against those who were thought to be possessed by evil spirits or cursed with the evil eye, or those wizards who presumed to contest the authority of the priests as the agents of Christ, such as Simon Magus, who was cast down from on high, according to Christian fable, because he dared to contest the magic of Christ.

Needless to say, the priests never characterized their power to work wonders as magic, yet it is difficult to know what else to call

it. In their narrow and irrational world, magic was forbidden. So what they did could never be magic, even though it might produce results identical to the actions of the wizards against whom they contested. Some of the saints could fly through the air, and when this happened it was a holy miracle; but if a magician should be seen to fly through the air, it was foul magic and the work of Satan. This was their logic, and practitioners of magic did not get very far trying to argue sense into them.

In a general sense, for the first twelve hundred years of Christian history, some forms of magic were condemned and other forms, although they might be prohibited in a technical sense, were tolerated or even engaged in by the priests themselves. Astrology was not strongly suppressed, and many Christian rulers, including Christian popes, depended on it for guidance. Similarly, leechcraft and various forms of healing magic were sought out by commoners who had no access to trained physicians, which was just as well, since the physicians of the Dark Ages killed their patients as often as they cured them. Worship of Pagan gods was forbidden by the priests, but again, it was not strenuously prosecuted for many centuries, because the early Church did not have the power to stamp out Pagan worship. The common people would have rebelled against the priesthood, and they knew it, so they tended to tread lightly when speaking out against the worship of Diana, goddess of witches.

The general consequence of these things is that the women we would think of today as witches—the rural wise women who healed the sick, divined the future, and sold love charms and fertility charms—were left to work their craft more or less unmolested. Around the year 1000 AD, the official Church penalty for the use of "witchcraft and enchantment" was a year on bread and water. It was not the most pleasant fate, but hardly tragic given the diet of the common folk at that time. Most witches were Christians, at least in a nominal sense. Natural magic was not considered a serious transgression of Church laws, but as the authority of the Church in Europe grew, so did its intolerance for religious dissent in all its forms. Greater power gave the Church a greater ability to exert its will over the people by the use of torture and execution. The Inquisition was instituted early in the reign of Pope Gregory IX (ruled from 1227 to 1241), known as the "Father of the Inquisition," to root out heretics.

During a period that extended roughly from the fifteenth to the seventeenth centuries, a strange madness swept across the face of Europe like a wind-driven wildfire that grew in strength with each passing generation. In his 1954 book *Witchcraft Today*, Gerald Gardner (often called the father of modern witchcraft) referred to this period as the "burning times," because being burned alive at the stake of was the customary form of execution used against heretics, including those accused of the crime of witchcraft.

In England, and much later in New England, a more civilized attitude prevailed and witches were only hanged; but in Scotland and on the Continent, they were often burned while still alive. Absurdly inflated estimates of the number of accused witches executed range from several hundred thousand to nine million, but a conservative estimate is that around 40,000 died, most of them women.

Whereas in previous centuries some kinds of magic had been tolerated and even practiced by the priests, during the burning times, all uses of magic in any form were seized upon by the inquisitors and witch-finders as proof that those who used them were nothing less than the bound servants of Satan himself. A kind of mythology that involved a black pact with the devil of witchcraft grew up in the writings of the demonologists in which the witch was supposed to have agreed to perform works of evil in return for prosperity, protection, and the power to work magic. It was elaborated in the testimonies of the witch trials, all of them extracted under the most extreme forms of physical torture, or the threat of torture.

Witches were saved from this madness by the dawning of the Age of Enlightenment, but even long before this general awakening of reason, there were a few courageous and forward-thinking men. Cornelius Agrippa and Reginald Scot, for example, began to speak out against the witch persecutions. They protested that the things witches were accused of by the inquisitors were impossible. Initially, these brave men were themselves persecuted by the priests as wizards and witches, but as more voices of reason joined theirs, the insanity of the witch-finders began to fall into disrepute among the educated class. The last dark flicker of the madness in America took place at Salem Village in 1692, with the hanging of eighteen men and women who were accused of witchcraft (one other poor old soul was pressed to death under rocks). Apart from a few isolated incidents after that, accused witches in Europe and the European colonies around the world were permitted to live.

When it became possible to practice magic openly in the 1950s, the modern witchcraft movement was born under the guiding hand of Gerald Gardner, an eccentric individual who had a passion for edged weapons and nudity, and who claimed to have been initiated into an existing witch coven in the New Forest in England in 1939. Witches today are indebted to Gardner for much of the underlying structure of both their craft and their religion. Gardner claimed that he had not invented the practices of modern witchcraft but was merely bringing into the open something that was already in existence in secret.

The angels that witches use in some of their rituals are the same angels that are used in ceremonial magic, and they are Christian angels.

Whatever the origin of Gardnerian witchcraft, whether it was composed by Gardner himself or simply the revelation of the teachings of a coven into which Gardner had been initiated, as Gardner always claimed, the system from which most other systems of modern witchcraft drew their strength and purpose was not created out of nothing. It was based solidly in Christian ceremonial magic, most notably the magic of the late nineteenth-century Rosicrucian society known as the Hermetic Order of the Golden Dawn.

Western ceremonial magic, or high magic as it is sometimes called, is a kind of *theurgy,* or "god magic." It was developed by Christian magicians within the context of Christian beliefs and practices. Although it has its roots in ancient Persia, Egypt, Greece, and the Pagan Roman Empire, the form we know today as ritual magic is very much a Christianized magic, and it has been for more than a thousand years. This shows itself most readily in the form of the numerous prayers that are used, which are directed at God and the angels of God, as these are named and recognized by Judaism and Christianity in the Old and the New Testaments of the Bible.

The angels that witches use in some of their rituals are the same angels that are used in ceremonial magic, and they are Christian angels. The best known are the archangels of the four directions of space, which in the Golden Dawn system of magic are Raphael (east), Michael (south), Gabriel (west), and Auriel (north). In the magic of today, these are known as the archangels of the four elements: air, fire, water, and earth. However, they are very ancient Christian angels whose names appear in New Testament, and in the Torah, which is the first five books and in the Old Testament. Christianity associates these archangels with the four heavenly creatures of the book of Revelation and with the four evangelists.

These four archangels of the quarters are used in the most fundamental ritual of the Golden Dawn, the Lesser Banishing Ritual of the Pentagram, which all beginners in that Rosicrucian society were taught. In this simple banishing ritual, banishing pentagrams of elemental earth are drawn upon the air at the four corners of a magic circle, and the four archangels invoked as guardians of their respective quarters. The pentagram is drawn in a specific way, which was originated by the Golden Dawn, and the elements that are assigned the four directions in a specific order were adopted by the Golden Dawn.

Every witch knows the importance of the pentagram, but how many know that it was first explicitly defined by the Golden Dawn? And how many know that Gerald Gardner adopted it for his own system of Gardnerian witchcraft from the Golden Dawn teachings, which he derived from various sources, including Aleister Crowley? The lesser banishing pentagram of earth, and its associated invoking pentagram of earth, are used in modern witchcraft extensively (see A *Witches' Bible* by Janet and Stewart Farrar [1996], pages 39 and 57, for images of these two pentagrams).

In that same text, which I mention because it is a well-respected handbook of witchcraft rituals and techniques of magic, the opening and closing rites that employ, respectively, the invoking and banishing pentagrams of earth mention the four watchtowers of the quarters. But how many witches know that the watchtowers are drawn from the system of angel magic taught to the Elizabethan magician John Dee by the Enochian angels at the end of the sixteenth century, or that they were an integral part of the Golden Dawn system? Similarly, the witchcraft practice of cleansing the magic circle with water and salt is also a Golden Dawn technique, somewhat modified. And the use of an altar within the circle, upon which is laid out the instruments of ritual, entered modern witchcraft from the Golden Dawn.

A hundred other links between the magical teachings of the Golden Dawn and those of modern witchcraft might be cited, were there space in this brief article to do so, and all of them would serve to show the debt that witchcraft, as it has descended from Gardner, owes to Christian ceremonial magic. Witches have taken the basic techniques and stripped from them their Christian names and allusions, which was a perfectly sensible and proper thing to do. In this way, witches have made these techniques their own. But in using them, and in seeking to truly understand them, witches should know where they originated.

There is an old popular saying, "Don't throw out the baby with the bath water." It means, don't discard something precious just to get rid of something disgusting. Another old axiom teaches us, "Don't cut off your nose to spite your face," meaning that we should not injure ourselves merely because we feel hostility toward someone else. It is worth bearing in mind that all the great European magicians of the Middle Ages were Christians. Many of them shared the same fate as witches—they were burned alive. However, they did not renounce their religion. They saw no conflict in believing in Christianity, and also at the same time practicing magic and communicating with spirits.

It was from the studies of these men (most of them were men, just as the majority of witches were women) that ceremonial magic, as it is preserved in the grimoires, evolved; and it was from this source that the system of the Golden Dawn was derived, which was the source Gardner used to build his vision of modern witchcraft. Modern witches are more closely tied to Christian magic than many of them know or would care to admit if they knew. Instead of rejecting the history of their craft, it would be better to understand its origins, and, in that way, to master it.

Donald Tyson *has written more than a dozen nonfiction books on Western occult subjects, such as divination, ceremonial magic, and the Kabbalah. He is also the author of a popular trilogy of works honoring H.P. Lovecraft, which include* Necronomicon, Alhazred, *and the* Necronomicon Tarot. *In his most recent book,* Runic Astrology, *Donald combines his knowledge of astrology and the runes to create a powerful new tool to use for divination.*

Illustrations by: Tim Foley

Should Pagans Pay for Rituals and Services?

Elizabeth Barrette

Raven: "Hey, you can't charge for running a ritual. It ruins the magic."
Morgan: "I have to pay the bills somehow. This is what I do well."

As the Pagan movement grows, different cultural expectations cause tension. Money is one of the controversial issues. Everyone has strong feelings about money and how it should, or should not, be spent. People disagree over whether magical and spiritual services should be paid for with money, or other forms of recompense, or if services should be provided with no expectation of return.

Our culture is not as young as it once was. We have second and third generation Pagans now, and we are growing into our place in this society. That's changing the way people relate to Pagan religions. We don't do things exactly like the old ways. What worked for our ancestors in their time and territory may not always work for us, but we can get good ideas from the old ways. The old ways do influence how we feel about money, magic, and spirituality, however, and we have to learn how to balance the old with the new to create a strong, functional, and sustainable Pagan way.

Background and Traditions

Historic cultures found different ways to meet their magical and spiritual needs. Their choices color our choices when we base our modern practices upon them. For example, some tribes supported a shaman who performed rituals for the people, interpreted visions, prayed, made charms, and so forth. As a specialist, the shaman collected a portion of food that the tribe hunted and gathered, and other people did most of the shaman's chores. Thus, the shaman could concentrate all time and energy on magical and spiritual matters instead of devoting effort to everyday tasks; it was the historic equivalent of being "on salary." Any tribe member could ask for the shaman's help without needing to pay for it in barter right then, because it was already covered; although people were often inspired to give extra presents in thanks for important tasks. This approach was fairly common among Native American cultures.

People donated coins or goods to the temple or shrine rather than pay an individual practitioner …

Another approach was the village witch. This person had an ordinary means of support, such as running a shop. Certain other services were also available, usually for barter, but occasionally for coin.

These included such things as love spells, divination, and laying protections. On the spiritual side, such a person might be in charge of a sacred well or stone circle, and assist visitors with blessings, prayers for healing, or purifications. This allowed the village witch to do magical and spiritual work as a sideline, the historic equivalent of working "part time" or "per item." It was a fairly popular technique in much of Europe until Christianity made a concerted effort to stamp it out.

Some cultures in the Middle East and parts of Europe established temples or shrines where magical and spiritual work could be done. Each had one or more keepers, some of whom served for a lifetime; others dedicated themselves for a certain time out of gratitude for a divine favor. These holy people organized festivals, cast spells for rain, and did other beneficial projects. People donated coins or goods to the temple or shrine rather than pay an individual practitioner, and rich people sometimes funded the construction of a new temple or shrine. This approach treated magical and spiritual services as a civic benefit, rather like modern-day firefighters.

In family traditions, one person might show particular talent for doing something, such as finding lost objects. The matriarch or patriarch of the family was consulted for all workings and customarily led magical and spiritual activities. For a magical family, these were as much a part of life as baking bread or repairing the house. Each person simply did what they were good at, or joined in group activities. In most cases, having general support of the family was enough. Even after Pagan religions faded from dominance, remnants lingered in many places.

All of those examples, along with others, contribute to our cultural background, and we need to consider them in the context of our modern discussions about appropriate exchanges. In particular, we need to consider that traditional practitioners often did not exchange for their services, but they did not work entirely "for free" either. Do any of these examples sound familiar to you?

Different societies had different economic systems. Native American cultures favored a gift economy, while much of Europe grew strong on barter. On a historic scale, our cash-dominant system is relatively new. While few contemporary Pagan paths directly continue those historic paths, almost all are largely inspired by them. We aim to recreate something similar to the magical and spiritual traditions of our ancestors, but we rarely try to copy the economic systems in which those traditions existed. That works out well enough in some situations, but it creates challenges in others, because the ancient concepts don't always fit smoothly when laid alongside modern ones.

Reasons to Pay

A modern economy runs mainly on money, more abstract than older forms of exchange such as barter. Outside our immediate circle of family and friends, most transactions involve money. We use cash or, even more abstract, credit to represent a certain amount of value; we earn money by working, then exchange it for desired goods or services, so it symbolizes the time and energy we use during that work. If you've ever used a coin or bill in a prosperity spell, you've taken advantage of the power in that symbol of value.

Some people consider money an acceptable form of energy exchange for magical/spiritual services. Some prefer barter, or a combination of cash and barter, as long as the officiate receives some kind of compensation for services. The reasons why people choose payment for magical/spiritual services include:

- The service requires specialized knowledge, skills, or materials to perform properly, meaning most people get better results by hiring an expert than by doing it themselves.

- Mainstream officiates charge for similar services, and clients generally expect to pay a fair market rate.

- The service requires time and/or effort that the officiate would not otherwise spend on that activity.

- The client does not have a suitable location for the service and wishes to use the officiate's space, or a public space.

- The service is not mentioned as a benefit of belonging to a spiritual group, or the client is a solitary practitioner.

- The magical/spiritual tradition of the client and the officiate allows or encourages compensation for such services.

- The officiate serves as part-time or full-time magical/spiritual support for a community and has obligations that make it difficult to make time for an activity unless it involves pay.

- The officiate has received formal training in the skills necessary for performing the service, which is an even stronger reason if the training involves tuition.

- The officiate has considerable experience in performing such services and/or has established a good rate of success.

- The client has plenty of money and uses it to conserve less plentiful personal resources, such as time, by hiring experts to perform services.

- The client wishes to contribute toward the support of the officiate and/or organization.

- The client and the officiate consider payment a convenient and appropriate form of energy exchange for this purpose.

Reasons Not to Pay

In today's economy, money is a concern for many people. The constant struggle to live comfortably and support a family can wear people down. It also tends to intrude on other parts of life, such as spirituality, and can become a serious distraction. There is even a popular, though not universal, belief that money has some kind of negative effect on magic. If you've ever gotten into an argument over money, you've seen the damage it can do.

In these reasons, some people prefer to keep money matters separate from magical/spiritual matters. Some traditions discourage or forbid members from paying for mystical services and from accepting such payment. Reasons against choosing payment for magical or spiritual services include:

- The service does not require specialized skills or knowledge; any reasonably careful person could do it.

- The officiate has only personal experience and general education to draw upon, not formal training related to the service.

- Mainstream officiates do not charge for similar services, because people either expect them for free or will perform such services for themselves.

- The service requires very little time, effort, or materials.

- The officiate would be doing a similar activity anyway.

- The service is included as a benefit of group membership.

- The service is included in the officiate's devotional duty to a higher power, performed free on appropriate occasions.

- The magical/spiritual tradition of the client and the officiate forbids or discourages compensation for such services.

- It is illegal to charge or pay for such services where participants live.

- The officiate has few or no outside obligations that would hinder performing the service for free.

- The officiate serves no official capacity and performs services when or if it is convenient.

- The officiate does not have a great deal of experience and/or has a variable rate of success.

- Many individuals who provide such services are disreputable and often defraud clients.

- The client has little or no money available.

- The client and the officiate consider payment an inconvenient, or inappropriate, means of energy exchange.

Magical and Spiritual Services

In theory, any sort of service could be done for money. In practice, certain things are customarily done for money, some are expected for free, and some are legally excluded from payment. Various magical and spiritual services span those categories. Some Pagan churches, like some mainstream churches, have established an official list of available services and the fee (if any) for each.

Probably the most common paid services are weddings and funerals. In the mainstream, officiates at these services usually charge a fee. Pagan officiates may charge a fee, which is typically reasonable. Some officiates perform these free for devotional reasons.

However, weddings and funerals share multiple features that incline people to pay for service: they are often large and complicated to plan; planning and performing these services requires much time and energy; they are very important; or the celebrants are likely to be overwhelmed by emotion and not up to handling logistics.

Fees are often charged for some services and for attendance at events. Public rituals and guest presentations will likely involve payment, especially when they are led by someone famous and experienced. A busy expert's time can command a respectable price. Also, people can pay to attend a ritual even if they don't belong to a coven or have access to public rituals. However, some events are free; even some paid events have free activities or charge only for admission.

Paying fees for divination is a seriously controversial arena. Divination is common in some places and illegal in others, and charging money for divination may be considered fraud. While some psychics and tarot readers have strong talent and ethics, others simply cheat people. Yet when practiced honestly, divination is an intense and tiring job; a good diviner definitely earns that payment. Tread cautiously in this area—find out the national, state, and local laws regarding paid or free divination. As a client, research diviners and choose someone you can trust. If you are a diviner, double-check the laws and communicate clearly with your clients about your stance on payment. Regarding divination, most New Age folks consider payment legitimate; Pagans are more divided. Always trust your instincts.

Spellcraft is even more controversial than divination. Magazines and Web sites often carry ads for pre-enchanted spell kits, or even spells to be performed by the officiate on behalf of the buyer. Most Pagan traditions, and many Pagan individuals, consider this very shady business as not necessarily evil, but easily and frequently misused. However, some traditions, such as Voudoun, consider it routine. Hiring an expert to perform a spell is their way of coping with a world that often stacks the deck against them. Some people feel that money distorts the magic of a spell and can make it go awry, which makes payment for spellcraft inadvisable. On the other hand, spellcraft is the service most likely to mean extra expenses for materials. Some people handle this with direct payment, while others stipulate the casting is free, but the client must provide any special materials for the officiate. (Few people are willing to spend money out of their own pocket to buy materials for a spell to benefit someone else.) Proportionally, very few reputable practitioners charge for spellcraft. Just the same, the field of paid spellcraft contains many charlatans. Apply the same guidelines as for divination, taking even more care in this rough territory. If something looks too good to be true, it probably is!

Methods of Recompense

While the contentious debate about paying or charging for Pagan services is often restricted to cash, there are other ways to exchange value. Even cash can be handled in assorted manners. Consider the details of a situation to figure out the best option for it. Possibilities include:

Pay-per-service: The client hires the officiate for a single activity and pays money for the service. This works well for clients who have more money than time, who aren't part of a magical community, and who need just this one thing done. Payment provides funds for those things (electric bill, grocery shopping, health care, etc.) that barter usually cannot cover; in a cash-dominant society, it is almost impossible to live without some cash.

Community support: Coven dues or other funds collected from a group often go toward supporting a mystical expert who performs magical or spiritual services for members of the group at no extra charge. A variation of this already in common use is "crediting" people's time for services on the coven's behalf against dues owed, so they don't have to pay cash dues. As Paganism grows, more people gravitate to the "congregation" model, which raises questions about the benefits of supporting dedicated part-time or full-time clergy, as most mainstream religions do. Like the pay-per-service model, this one also provides some cash for mundane essentials that other types of exchange cannot cover.

Barter: Instead of exchanging money for services, people trade services or goods they have for different services or goods they want. This allows exchange when money is scarce and avoids potential clashes over mixing money and magic/religion; it also helps everyone feel useful, while still balancing the equation so that one person doesn't get something for free at someone else's expense. The main disadvantage to barter is that it requires complementary needs, because exchange is only possible if both people have something the other wants. Another disadvantage is most bills must be paid in cash rather than barter, so barter can't accomplish everything in a cash-dominant economy. Barter works well in a larger community in which people can mix and match their needs.

> **Whether you mix money and magic should be a considered choice, not taken for granted based on outside advice.**

Favor trading: In close-knit families, small groups, and covens, people do things for each other all the time without expecting anything specific in return. This is less explicit than barter, and a healthy relationship will balance out the energy investment over time. When it works, this method is comfortable and builds strong bonds. The drawback is that it requires a relationship with other people in order to work at all. If some people regularly give more than they receive (and vice versa, for other people), serious dysfunction may result. Have you ever met someone who always needs a favor but never helps anyone else? Energy vampires can drain a whole group this way. Like barter, favor trading also cannot cover all needs in a cash-dominant economy. However, this option remains popular among many small Pagan groups.

Considerations and Decisions

Whether you mix money and magic should be a considered choice, not taken for granted based on outside advice. First, know yourself and your beliefs. Second, study your magical/spiritual tradition and its stance (if any) on this issue. Third, consider the particular situation and whether it leans one way or the other. What will work for you, under what circumstances, and why?

Realize that you are ultimately responsible for your own beliefs, actions, and ethics. If you disagree with the mainstream, or with tenets of your own tradition, the choice is up to you. Also include your experiences, both good and bad. You may find that paying or charging for magical/spiritual services works for you, or you may find that it does not. Then again, you may discover that it works in some situations but not others, or that direct payments cause problems but other forms of exchange work fine.

Finally, strive for grace in debating this issue with other people. Their experiences or traditions may have led them to different conclusions than yours. That's okay. You can discuss facts, anecdotes, and principles without yelling at each other. In truth, it's not money that's the root of all evil; it's selfishness.

Resources

Dickinson, K. "Avoiding Pagans for Profit: 12 Red Flags." Thrice Taboo Spiritual Community. http://www.thricetaboo.com/avoid.html (retrieved July 10, 2009).

Gold, Peter. "What I Expect from My Church." The Cauldron: A Pagan Forum. http://www.ecauldron.net/opedexpect.php (retrieved July 10, 2009).

Orr, Emma Restall. *Living With Honour.* Berkeley, CA: O Books, 2008.

Slaney, Clare. "Pagan Generosity." Pagan Chaplaincy. http://Paganchaplaincy.blogspot.com/2009/06/Pagan-generosity.html (retrieved July 10, 2009).

Wigington, Patti. "Should You Pay For Spellcasting Services? Wading Through The World of Internet Wicca." http://Paganwiccan.about.com/od/magicandspellwork/a/payforspells.htm (retrieved July 10, 2009).

Wood, Robin. *When, Why . . . If.* Westland, MI: Robin Wood Enterprises, 1997.

Elizabeth Barrette *has been involved in the Pagan community for more than twenty years. Her other writing fields include speculative fiction and gender studies.*

Illustrator: Paul Hoffman

Conferring Celebrity Status on "Big Name Pagans"

Boudica

The expression "Big Name Pagan" (also known as BNP) is tossed around a lot at Pagan events. Usually, the BNP is a well-known author who is speaking about a book or personal experiences. And sometimes it's the Pagan band that is playing (they even have their groupies). Many Pagans will also travel to an event to purchase a piece of art or look at new work created by their favorite community artist.

While these authors and artists are not mainstream celebrities, we do have a tendency to hold some of our own authors, community leaders, musicians, and artists in the same high esteem we reserve for mainstream celebrities. We often give our Pagan celebrities a special kind of influence over us that you do not extend to conventional authors or artists. This is as dangerous as it is enchanting, because this is a spiritual path that we follow. This phenomenon happens in other religious communities, too. For example, people traveled long distances to hear Billy Graham speak. (Mr. Graham's speeches were free to attend, by the way, and donations were optional.) While this phenomenon is not unique to the Pagan culture, it does provide interesting discussion when examined a bit more closely.

Who are Celebrity BNPs?

A celebrity is a well-known person. How do we know these people? Mostly, we know them from their works. These people are perceived as the movers and shakers within our community and role models for our cultural and spiritual practices.

It seems we need role models that we can look up to, especially in the Pagan community. Many practitioners will never have a real "in person" spiritual teacher; the book in their hands may be the only way they will come to know their path, and the author who wrote the book becomes the person they lean on for what they need spiritually. This can present some dilemmas for authors and practitioners alike if practitioners become too reliant on their "Pagan celebrities," especially if practitioners come to rely more upon the experiences of the author rather than on their own spiritual experiences.

But in the Pagan community, the phenomenon can become more like a three-ring circus, depending on the event and the speaker or band. I've seen BNPs walk through an event with a small crowd of followers right on their coat tails. They seem to only beckon and people fall in line. A BNP's followers will oftentimes mimic the headwear or dress of their BNP leader; it is as comical as it is sad.

To allow someone to influence you to the point of losing your originality is like allowing yourself to become part of a cult. This can be a sign of some type of emotional illness. Individuals need to exercise control, but if the BNP allows and even encourages this kind of behavior, it suggests that there is something wrong with the BNP as well.

Then, there are events where people pay big bucks to sit in an auditorium to hear their favorite author weave stories about personal experiences and magical happenings for the audience. These speakers want to empower the people in their audiences and workshops.

Real Celebrities

I remember the first time I met Dorothy Morrison. We had corresponded in e-mails, and in our exchanges, Dorothy sounded like a very sharp woman, on the ball, and part of today's culture. Even so, when she handed me her registration at the reception table at Blessed Be and Meet Me in Washington D.C., she was not what I had expected. The southern drawl, her very tasteful clothing, and her perfectly done hair and makeup were atypical of most of the "witchy" people in our community. Dorothy's appearance was a refreshing change from the pale skin, dark hair, and caked makeup of other witches I had so far encountered. The professional witch could not be differentiated from the professional woman.

She did an impromptu workshop for our benefit, and never once did she tout centuries of oppression or the Burning Times. Instead, she discussed the here and now, personal empowerment from our deities today, and how to make magic work for us now! Oh, it was so refreshing, so wondrous coming from a twenty-first-century witch.

Dorothy *is* a Pagan celebrity! She is an integrated part of our communities, not someone to point at and be amused by. She is someone worth investigating further.

I ran into Kerr Cuhulain at that same event. I had just picked up my dinner and was waiting for the rituals on the Mall to begin. Someone had forgotten to get food for Kerr, and I shared my Chinese meal with him. We talked about the differences between Canadian police and police from larger urban centers, like New York and Los Angeles. When he discussed what he did for a living, he spoke deliberately and the discussion was serious—and he wore a jacket and tie! As we talked about the event and the people we were meeting, the discussion became more lighthearted. It was a great "getting to know you" session. Later, at his workshop, he projected the same kind of persona to his audience, and people listened as he spoke about being a warrior in the Pagan path. He didn't preach. Instead, he discussed the Pagan path in the here and now. He is another person I could call a Pagan celebrity. It's possible to get some kind of feeling for the type of people they are from reading their books. But nothing says it better than meeting  them in person. That's when you really get to know them.

It was also a pleasure to meet and talk with Kristen Madden, and her workshops are always a delight to attend. She comes prepared, she listens to questions and addresses the members of her workshop personally. She is just as lovely a person as you can imagine. Her books are as gentle and informative as she is; they are reflective of someone who has done the research and who shares her experiences honestly.

I have to mention that I ran into Tannin Schwartzstein, coauthor of *Urban Primitive* and other titles since then. She was setting up her vending table, and we got some chances to talk one-on-one during the event. Although we are from different generations and very different cultures, I found her to be intelligent, interesting, well-spoken, and very much part of, and in touch with, her own cultural base. It was a pleasure to talk with her. Our discussions stood out as memorable, and well above some of the other discussions I had that weekend with some other so-called BNPs.

Some are Celebrities, but Shouldn't Be

I've met a few well-known authors and artists over the years whom I hope never to meet again. While their books are full of information, meeting these people in person made me wonder how they managed to sell their book to anyone! Some BNPs have such nasty dispositions, and are so needy and so "above" everyone else that it is hard to imagine how they could ever convince anyone that their spiritual life is worth emulating.

I've met and worked with some very unreliable BNPs who would promise to do an event and never show up, or they showed up and I would wish they hadn't. Some of these people look like they have been on a month-long binge, and then their "handler" remembered the engagement, scooped them out of the gutter and dropped them off at the hotel or park. Others have been so crass as to suggest that they be provided with a "companion" for the night.

What we read in the books by our favorite authors, or what we see in the art painted by an artist, or hear in the music of our favorite Pagan bands is not necessarily reflective of the person behind the work. Some of these people are professional authors or artists who know what the public wants and they attempt to give it to them. But there is no guarantee that they practice what they preach, and this is where we tend to get into trouble. We idolize our celebrities and take it for granted that these people know what they are doing or what they are talking about, and therefore we follow them—sometimes blindly. We are so accustomed to being entertained by professionals that we sometimes have trouble differentiating between entertainers and spiritual practitioners. We seem to have a difficult time telling who is living in our communities and who is living off of our communities.

I have heard a lot of things about Selena Fox over the years, some of it good, some of it not so good. Selena has made her mark in the Pagan world by fostering several organizations that have done consistently well in purpose as well as financially. But for every success, there are those who will say things about her, because—well,

I think they are jealous more often than not. My own experiences with Selena suggest that she is a very experienced businesswoman. She has her sights set on success and knows how to achieve it. Working with her on the Pagan Headstone Campaign gave me some insights into who this woman is and how she works. And believe me, she works! She gives more than lip service to the Pagan community. She puts her heart into it, and my experience working with her has been nothing but positive. Selena has left a very positive mark on the Pagan community.

The first time I met M. R. Sellars, he was standing outside a store in Columbus, a cigar in one hand, a flask of scotch in the other. He had a long pony-tail and wore a flak jacket. I was enchanted by him the moment I saw him, and he has proven to be not only a really great mystery writer, but also a "roll up your sleeves" community worker as well.

Get to Know the BNPs before You Celebrate Them

In all communities, you have the good and the bad, and the Pagan community is no exception. As we watch authors, artists, and musicians come and go in our community, we need to really get to know who they are and see if they really deserve the celebrity status we tend to automatically bestow on them. What we need to do is to learn how to separate our spirituality and culture from that of the people who help us with our everyday practices.

We need to remember that these people are exactly that—people. There are those who have the ability to be a role model if we would like to think of them as such. There are most definitely Pagan celebrities who deserve the attention we lavish on them. But again, we must remember that they are not personal counselors, they are not psychiatric practitioners, and they cannot solve all our problems for us. They are human, they can make mistakes, and they put their pants on one leg at a time. They can be cultural icons as long as we do not elevate them to the status of a god. We know from our history what happens when we endow mere mortals with god-like qualities. We end up shooting ourselves in the foot.

We have some really wonderful Pagan celebrities in our community. We have others who maybe we should get to know better. And the best way to do that is to meet them in person, listen to them speak, and follow what they DO, not just what they say. Actions have always spoken louder than words.

Boudica *is the reviews editor and co-owner of the* Wiccan/Pagan Times *and owner of the* Zodiac Bistro, *both online publications. She is a high priestess with the Mystic Tradition Teaching Coven of Pennsylvania, Ohio, New Jersey, New York, and Maryland. Boudica is frequently a guest speaker at local and East Coast events. A former New Yorker, she now resides with her husband and six cats in Ohio.*

Illustrator: Bri Hermanson

Magic Christians

Donald Tyson

C hristian fundamentalists will sometimes try to drive a wedge between
ordinary Christians and those people—
witches and druids, for example—who
follow more esoteric or occult paths
to spiritual fulfillment. Christians are
warned that any and all forms of New
Age teachings must avoided; that Satan
himself lurks in the Ouija board and
the tarot cards; and that divination, astrology, channeling, meditation, yoga,
and, indeed, every esoteric path leads
straight to hell. The ignorance of fundamentalist writers such as Hal Lindsey,
Derek Prince, and others concerning

these subjects is astonishing. They literally do not know the slightest thing about witchcraft, magic, the occult, or the paranormal. Yet, because the average Christian is equally unfamiliar with these subjects, many are intimidated.

Fortunately, not all Christians fall into the fundamentalist mindset. There is a growing movement across Christianity to reconnect with the Goddess, with the rhythms and needs of the planet and the matching rhythms of their own bodies, and with the empowering practice of magic. I call these seekers after spiritual awakening "magic Christians."

Modern witches who tend to be hostile toward Christianity and Christians, because of the persecutions against witchcraft, should stop to consider this yearning within the hearts of many Christians for meaning on a personal level and have compassion for those who genuinely seek the magical sources of their faith. Not all Christians are automatically hostile to Paganism; some do actively seek to breathe new life into the aridity and doctrinal rigidity of both Catholicism and Protestant denominations.

One way this yearning for meaning reveals itself is in the worship of the Virgin Mary, a practice known as Mariolatry, which has always been discouraged by the priesthood of Rome. While the priesthood may view the worship of a woman as a threat to their all-male authority, Mariolatry itself is very popular today in Spain and in the Spanish-speaking nations of the Americas.

The early bishops of the Church excluded the female sex and expressed the Divine Trinity as an all-male concept. While many people might think that the Holy Spirit is sexless, neither male nor female, the New Testament refers to the Holy Spirit with the masculine pronoun, even though *pneuma*, the word for "spirit," is neither male nor female. Just one example from the King James translation of the Bible will show you what I mean. In John 16:13, it was written, "when he, the Spirit of truth, is come, he will guide you into all truth."

> **Those who make Mary the main object of their active worship regard her as a living vessel for the Holy Spirit. Indeed, she is another form of the Goddess of witchcraft, the great universal mother principle, the divine feminine . . .**

This strikes those of us who are involved in alternative spiritual practices as absurd. How can God be distinguished into three parts, a father part, a male child part, and some sort of weird masculine energy—an uncle part, perhaps? Yet, there is no Mother part. If there is no feminine aspect to God, how was God the Son born?

Well, needless to say, Christian theologians have tried to explain this for centuries, and I will not even attempt to get into their arguments. But I will point out that it struck many Christians of past ages as absurd, even as it does us in our modern age, and they responded by creating—outside the authority of the bishops—a kind of unofficial feminine component of God, which is the Virgin Mary, mother of Jesus. Worship of the Virgin became so popular that the popes were forced to permit it, since they could not stamp it out.

Worshipping the Mother

Those who make Mary the main object of their active worship regard her as a living vessel for the Holy Spirit. Indeed, she is another form of the Goddess of witchcraft, the great universal mother principle, the divine feminine that pervades and animates all things. Mary is not merely honored, in an abstract way, as the mother of Jesus, she is directly worshipped and adored in her own right as a compassionate and nurturing deity who listens as a loving mother to the prayers of her children. Shrines to Mary are innumerable throughout Mexico, Guatemala, Ecuador, and all the Latin American nations. It is the elevation of Mary to the rank of goddess that the all-male priesthood of Rome finds so intolerable, because Mary puts a human, feminine face on the third part of the Trinity.

As witches know, the Goddess wears many faces. Recently, another aspect of the Divine Mother has emerged among magic Christians. It is Mary Magdalene, who has become popularized in several books, one being Dan Brown's novel *The Da Vinci Code*, and another the nonfiction work *Holy Blood, Holy Grail* by Baigent, Leigh, and Lincoln. In these and other works, a theory is set forth that Jesus had a wife, and from the womb of this woman issued a child, or children, who are the direct descendants of Christ. The belief is that this bloodline did not die out but still exists today. Mary Magdelene is usually the woman identified as the wife of Jesus. There is significance in the reappearance of the name Mary, because it shows that the Goddess, in the form of the mother of Christ, has resurfaced in the person of the wife of Christ and mother of his children. She is still the divine Creatrix.

Angel Magic

Another clear sign of the ongoing spiritual quest among magic Christians is their current fascination with angels. Countless books have been written over the past decade or so concerning the nature of angels, and ways to draw upon their power for help in daily life. This is angel magic, a type of magic that has existed for many centuries in the Western esoteric tradition. The occult aspects of angel worship are downplayed in Christian books due to the prohibition of all forms of magic by fundamentalists.

Witches have always kept familiar spirits and used magic to communicate with the spirits and lesser deities of the natural world. In Catholicism, these roles are filled, sometimes awkwardly and imperfectly, by angel messengers. Christian worshippers use these angel messengers as intermediaries between themselves and God.

As much as the clergy would like to distance itself and the people from angel worship, it still goes on in Latin countries and places around the world. Angel statues or portraits are placed into household shrines, where they receive daily prayers and offerings. The reason for the popularity of this intermediate adoration is not difficult to fathom. Christians find it awkward to seek help in some minor personal matter from the impersonal God of the universe, who after all is the God of all people and all things, but it is easy to imagine that an angel with whom the believer has formed a close personal bond will listen and respond.

Angels, the messengers of God, are intermediaries that serve the same function as the witches' familiars and spirit guides. At one time it was believed that every Christian had two personal angels who never departed—a good angel who stood behind the right shoulder, and an evil angel who stood behind the left shoulder. Sometimes the evil angel was not spoken about, and reference was made only to a holy guardian angel who watched over the human being's life. In modern occultism, the best-known form of angel magic is the prolonged and complex ritual working in the grimoire known as the *Book of the Sacred Magic of Abramelin the Mage*. The ritual is used to establish a communication between the magician and his or her holy guardian angel, a link that endures thereafter throughout the life of the magician.

The saints, another intermediary class of spiritual beings, are worshipped with great enthusiasm among traditional Catholics, especially in Spanish-speaking countries, where shrines have a place in countless households. The saints are a form of sacred ancestor, very similar to the *loas*, voodoo gods. The voodoo gods are based on great ancestors who have become so potent, magically, that they have ascended to the rank of deities. There are lesser ancestor spirits in voodoo who are kept in vessels by descendants related to them by bloodlines. The great spirits who are the gods were also once men and women, although this is not always understood.

There is a natural tendency to elevate the reputation and stature of the revered dead until they ascend through the rank of legendary heroes to demi-gods, and finally to the exalted status of full gods. We see these stages of exaltation in the various forms of the Pagan Greek Herakles (Hercules to Romans). Herakles began as a man, or so anthropologists believe, but after his death, he became the subject of myths that portrayed him as semi-divine. Eventually, he was regarded as one of the gods. The same process, which is universal

among many religions, has occurred with the saints of Catholicism. But because the doctrines of the Church deny the existence of any god other than the one Christian God, the saints have been frozen in status below the rank of full gods. Even so, Christians who seek magical aid and protection often treat the saints they adore and worship as deities, which raises the ire of the priests.

Magic Christians seek the active intervention of saints in their lives in the form of miracles. This often is done by petitioning a particular saint thought to have authority and office in the area of life pertaining to the desired miracle. For example, the patron saint of lost causes is St. Jude, the patron saint of travel is St. Christopher, and so on. Witches will recognize in these offices the similar roles assigned to various spirits and gods in Paganism. Artemis is goddess of the hunt, Ceres provides bountiful harvests, Hades is lord of the dead—each deity has his or her specific function.

When witches seek intervention by a god, they make an offering; when Catholics seek intervention by the appropriate saint, they also makes offerings in the form of prayers and observances. Often, the Christian will strike a personal bargain with the saint and in return for the miracle, the Christian will agree to perform some penance or task, or give up some precious possession or enjoyment as a form of sacrifice. Now and then, such bargains between believer and saint appear in the classified sections of newspapers. This is done as a way of formalizing the bargain. Needless to say, it is a magic act.

Such pacts with saints are always magical in nature. There is no other term to describe them. The saints are believed to act in harmony with the will of God but still on their own authority and judgment. It is a personal agreement, or contract, between an individual Christian worshipper and a specific saint who is capable of supplying the desired miracle. Very close bonds are formed with the saints.

Worshippers actually converse with their images, and as a result those images become animated in a magical way, just as the statues of gods and goddesses in Pagan Greece and Rome became animated by worship. When the image of a saint becomes animated, it will appear to the worshipper to respond to his or her words and emotions. This is an extremely ancient phenomenon, and it still goes on today because it is universal and cuts across all major religions and historic periods, cultures, and geographical regions.

Witches are known for their power of seership (the seeing of visions in mirrors, crystals, water, tea leaves, tarot cards, and other divinatory media). Christians who have reawakened their magical

spirituality are more apt to receive visions in the form of apparitions and dreams, but sometimes Jesus, or the Virgin Mary, will appear. Angels are credited with conveying these visions, or enabling their occurrence.

The Visions of Fátima, a famous series of Christian visions, were received by three children at Fátima, Portugal, in the year 1917. The Virgin Mary appeared to the children on the thirteenth day of the month for six months in a row. One of the children, Lúcia Santos, described her appearance as "brighter than the sun." Needless to say, the Virgin Mary was a manifestation of the Goddess. In return for these visions, the children performed various acts that served as sacrifices to Mary. They refrained from drinking water for periods of time, tied cords tightly around their waists until they cut into their flesh and caused discomfort, and did other acts of penance. We see here the familiar pattern of the magical bargain—the penance was payment for the visions.

Thus far, we have examined only some of the magical practices of Catholics, but Protestant Christians in America of various denominations, even those who are under the forbidding influence of Fundamentalism, still find ways to express their faith magically. One way is by faith healing. Jesus was famous even in his own lifetime as a healer of the sick. Protestants are able to channel his occult energies through their own bodies and, in this way, to become healers by proxy. They invoke the name of Jesus when they heal, whereas a witch would invoke the Goddess, but the principle is the same, and the action of the magic identical.

Magic Christians of Protestant denominations also speak in tongues, a practice less common among Catholics. They believe that the Holy Spirit descends upon them just as it did upon the disciples of Christ on the day of the Pentecost, following the execution of Christ on the cross. This is a form of spirit possession. Often the words of the spirits who possess the believers are incoherent, but sometimes clear instructions or predictions of the future are received. Charismatic Christian worshippers who have received the Holy Spirit and have spoken in tongues would probably be disturbed to know that they are doing the same thing that channelers and spirit mediums do, but so it is.

Modern witches and Pagans should have patience for these magic Christians who, even though they yearn for direct spiritual union with the Goddess and her servants, still deny the suggestion that what they do is a form of magic. They only fear the word, not the practice itself, because they have been taught to fear and hate it. Their teachers are ignorant, and their fear is a form of ignorance. With gentle persuasion, many of them can be led to the understanding that they worship and commune with the same goddess that witches, druids, magicians, and all those grouped under the umbrella term New Age worship.

Donald Tyson's *bio appears on page 27.*

Illustrator: Rik Olson

Witchy Living

Day-by-Day Witchcraft

Magic in the Net

Jenett Silver

It's easy to forget all the ways we can connect online and the many choices that are available to enrich our spiritual or magical practice. If it has been a while since you explored the Internet, or you want to learn more about it and and about connecting with other magical people, I've prepared a short Internet primer for you.

Getting Started

There are a few commonsense guidelines that apply when anyone goes online to find other people who are interested in Paganism and magic. First,

online spaces and tools change rapidly. What is hot and new right now will change by next year. Expect to spend a little time in ongoing learning. Local libraries have resources to help you with new tools, and community centers and adult education programs often offer inexpensive computer classes. A friendly high school or college student can be a great resource as well.

Second, it helps to know what you're looking for. Some Web sites focus on sharing information, while others spend more time on social chat. Some places encourage debate and discussion, even when it gets heated, while others want everyone to get along. Some sites have many different kinds of people and interests represented, and others are focused on a specific topic.

A simple search can turn up many different pages about almost any topic from historical herbals, ancient calendars, deity information, to spells, magical advice, astrology, and tarot.

Third, you'll enjoy some people and spaces more than others. If a space isn't the right fit for you, move on. Sometimes people may become rude or nasty, and common sense (like disengaging from them) will get you through most issues. It often helps to take a walk or sleep on an issue before responding, but if you need more help with a problem, such as ongoing harassment, most sites have tools and offer assistance.

Finally, remember that anything you post online is effectively public. With the rise in social networking sites, many people try searches on the names of people they know. If you don't want your coworkers, neighbors, or others in your life to know about your religious or spiritual preferences, or you want to tell them directly yourself, be careful. Avoid using your legal name or other identifying information, including a photo, online when you're talking about those topics. Always respect other people's privacy by checking with them before you use their name, or before you upload photos or videos of them in ritual or magical settings.

Finding Your Way

A good place to start is with search engines and how they are used to find sites and information online. You'll be able to find the things you're most interested in far more easily once you know how to search.

Get familiar with tagging. Tagging allows people to identify something on a Web site—a post, a photo, or a video, for example— by using a word or short phrase. For example, a public ritual for Samhain that included a spiral dance might have the tags "ritual," "Samhain," and "spiral dance." If you enter any of those tags in the search box, you could click on any of them to find other items on that site, or from person who posted it, with those tags.

Remember that each site will work a little differently. Many sites offer an introductory tour or tutorial to help you get started. Other users will also write up guides that you can find with a quick search. Try this: combine a site name you are familiar with and terms like "FAQ," "introduction," or "tutorial."

Check around the site you are interested in to locate any rules for using the site, and become familiar with those rules.

Information

One common reason people look online is to find information. And of course, there's also plenty of information about different paths, groups, and practices. Authors and publishers share information about their books online, which can help you make wise choices about resources.

An author (or group of authors) may share links to other interesting sites, news, personal experiences, or many other kinds of resources on a blog. Most also have a place for comments so you can talk with the author of the post or others who are interested in that specific topic. These give a more personal way to explore different topics.

One site worth mentioning is Witch's Voice at http://witchvox.com. It is one of the oldest Pagan and magical networking sites on the Internet. Through user submissions, they maintain a international database of groups, events, stores, and personal listings (among others) for the Pagan and magical community. If you want to locate people in your physical area, it's a great place to start looking.

Of course, keep your brain engaged. People can claim all sorts of experience or credentials online that might or might not be true. There can also be reasons something would not be a good fit for you personally. Check out anything that sounds unusual, or that you plan to put in or on your body (herbs, incense, and so forth). Make sure the product and/or resource is reliable before you take the next step and buy or submit your personal information.

Groups of Like-minded People

You can find groups discussing Paganism, magic, Wicca, witchcraft, or many other topics in every format. If you like e-mail, search for e-mail lists (many are on Yahoo! Groups at http://groups.yahoo.com. There are Web-based forums, where you go to a Web site and interact there. Many social networking sites, such as Facebook at http://facebook.com and MySpace at http://myspace.com, allow users to create discussion groups or other connections within the site.

Finding a great online group can take some practice. Look for groups with at least five to fifteen meaningful comments or posts a day (this is a sign of ongoing active conversation). Choose groups that have a good mix of people. When some are new to the subject and others have more experience, it usually results in better information and more perspective. Read through past posts to get an idea of how the group works and whether there are regular posters whose comments are especially helpful to you.

Also, consider your available time. A large group can produce dozens of messages every day. You may want to read only some topics or catch up once a week in some cases. In others, you may decide to check in frequently so that you can participate in the conversation.

Hearing and Seeing

Current technology makes it very easy to share sound and video files. Sites like YouTube (http://youtube.com) include everything from videos of public rituals to tips on how to make tools, candles, or other crafts. You can even find video trailers for books! Flickr (http://flickr.com) allows you to share photos and other images, and to find images other people have posted (like altars, magical art, or photos of famous mystical places like Stonehenge).

Sites can also connect you to great music. MySpace made its name connecting bands with listeners, and still gives a great way to check out all kinds of music, including many Pagan and magical artists. Podcasts (audio recordings similar to radio shows) cover every topic under the sun, and there are a number focusing on magic, Paganism, or other related topics. Try a search for "podcast" and the subject you're interested in, or search for "podcast directory" and do some browsing. Finally, services such as Pandora (http://pandora.com) find music for you based on similarities to music you select (like an artist or album).

If you're looking to learn the tune for a chant, many sites have recordings of common ritual chants (and some less common ones). A search on the chant name or the first line of the lyrics will sometimes find you a recording. And, of course, musicians and artists often have samples on their Web sites.

New and Innovative

One constant about the Internet is change. Each year brings new technologies, resources, and ways to use them that have never been done before. Take microblogging, where users make very short posts using a tool like Facebook and Twitter (http://twitter.com) to share brief (140 character) comments about their lives or what they're thinking. Microbloggers share links, ideas, inspirations, and moments in their day.

Virtual worlds are also on the rise. Some are games, such as World of Warcraft, but other virtual spaces allow you to create and explore a world. One of the best known is Second Life (http://secondlife.com), where there are many different Pagan and magical groups who do

rituals, celebrations, and other activities together. Users have recreated public spaces like museums, pyramids, and all sorts of other locations that would be hard to visit in person. As technology improves, these virtual worlds become even deeper and people more immersed in them.

Many Options

There are dozens of ways you can use technology to deepen your spiritual and religious life. Check these out, but also explore on your own. Try terms like "Pagan," "witch," or "magic," or the place where you live, to see a little of what's out there on the Internet.

Publishers (including Llewellyn, of course) are using social networking to connect with readers. Content includes new releases, spell-of-the-day links, and links to interesting articles or blogs.

Some events encourage live blogging. You can follow comments about workshops, panels, and other activities even if you can't be there. These often include books or other resources that presenters have mentioned.

Explore the creative powers of social networking. Poetry, retellings of myths, short stories, and all sorts of other art forms come out every day. Try out your own!

Whether you're passionate about local foods, saving endangered species, making your community a better place to live, or any other topics, there are others who are interested in the same things. Social networking sites make it easy to find like-minded people and share resources for your cause.

Do you pick a tarot card of the day? Online sites do this as well and encourage discussion by asking people to respond with ideas or how that card or rune fits their day.

Check out sites for your other hobbies. If you knit, crochet, or spin yarn to make magical items, check out Ravelry (http://ravelry.com) to find Pagan and myth-focused groups and projects. You can find similar sites for food, music, art, and many other hobbies.

Do you have a daily intention? Use a microblogging tool, like Facebook or Twitter, to share it with others. Your friends can help support your goals.

Every Use Counts

The simplest acts can reinforce your goals. Does your work require you to change passwords regularly? Pick a password that reflects your current spiritual or magical goal. When I was working on getting a professional library job, I used passwords like "prosperity," "success," and "fruition" that helped remind me of my goal every time I logged in.

Decorate your electronic space. Explore the wide range of digital images, photographs, and other ways to make your computer desktop unique. You can even change your icons to remind you of your goals. My writing program has an icon of a fountain pen to remind me to write thoughtfully. You can use "user pictures" or icons on online sites to reflect your goals and priorities, too. I use an edited image

of my harp in many places to remind me of the power of music in my life.

And, of course, keep your life balanced. It can be tempting to spend all our free time online, exploring many delightful options (it certainly is for me). But I know that's not the only thing I want to do. I also want to bake, play my harp, go for a walk, have dinner with friends, and do ritual work on my own and with my coven.

I regularly check in with myself about my online time. I make sure it still feels balanced and meaningful to me. If it doesn't, I figure out what would help. Whatever you decide, know that you can always make changes. Just because one online site is the perfect place for you now doesn't mean you need to keep being there for the next year, especially when it has become boring or frustrating. And there's always the chance a new site or resource will come along that will have an even better combination of features that suit your needs and desires.

There truly is magic in the pixels. Find where it leads you, and enjoy the ride.

Jenett Silver *is a witch in the Twin Cities and a priestess in a coven with a strong focus on music and the arts in ritual. A librarian by profession, she can generally be found with her nose in a book or at the computer. Her blog can be found at http://gleewood.org/threshold.*

Illustrator: Neil Brigham

My Top 3 Rules for Pagan Living

Deborah Blake, Dallas Jennifer Cobb
& Susan Pesznecker

Deborah Blake

One of the great things about being a witch is that there aren't a lot of rules. Most Pagans tend to be free spirits who choose this path because they don't like being told what to do or how to think.

On the other hand, my experience over the last thirteen years or so, since I set my own feet on the Pagan path, is that most folks—whether they call themselves Wiccans, witches, or Pagans—tend to share a few major beliefs. You might even go so far as to call them Pagan rules.

Okay. Don't everyone start yelling at me at once. You'll scare the cats, for goddess' sake. I'm not saying that every Pagan believes in or follows these rules. I have yet to find anything that every single witch I know agrees on. Nor am I telling you that you have to follow these rules. Each witch must decide for him- or herself which of these beliefs resonates as "truth."

However, if you are dedicated to living your life the Pagan way, it is a good idea to know what your peers consider the rules to be. And it never hurts to have an answer when some nonPagan asks you, "What do witches believe in, anyway?"

The Wiccan Rede: An It Harm None, Do As Ye Will

Whether a witch considers herself to be a Wiccan (and many do not), most witches follow the Harm None rule. Simply put, it states that you may do whatever you wish, so long as, in doing it, you are not harming anyone.

Of course, you will find that it is not so simple after all if you look at this rule more closely. For one thing, there is no way to predict which actions might eventually lead to harm, although sometimes it is obvious. If you purposely run over someone's foot with your car, for instance, that will most assuredly harm them. But what if you refuse to give your friend a ride when they ask for one, and they get in an accident in the taxi on the way home? Did you cause harm?

No, that one is not your fault. The difference here is in your intention. The law of Harm None (to my mind, at least) is about not causing intentional harm either to yourself or to others. Oh, yes, it applies to your actions toward yourself, too. (Put the potato chips down.)

This rule is even more important when you are talking about the use of magick. As witches, we know that we can use the power of magick to affect the world around us. Hopefully, we use that power to create positive change in our lives.

For me, Harm None is the most important rule of all, and it leads directly to the other two. While I realize that many people find it acceptable to use the powers of magick to harm others, especially those whom they believe "deserve it," I have to disagree. I am not so wise or so all-seeing that I can be certain of who does or doesn't deserve to be punished for their misdeeds. I am happy to leave such weighty choices up to the gods, and trust in the second rule—the Law of Returns—to take care of such things for me.

The Law of Returns

The Law of Returns is fairly simple: what you put out into the world is what you will get back. This belief isn't limited to Pagans, either. Some witches go so far as to call it the Threefold Law and believe that everything comes back to us times three. So if you donate money to a good cause, you might get a winning lotto ticket. Kick an old homeless guy—well, watch out!

I don't worry too much about whether what I put out into the universe comes back to me once or three times. I do try to be careful to put out positive thoughts, words, and actions, however, and I avoid negative ones. You can see how this ties in to the rule to harm none. If you walk around harming others, that harm is likely to come back to you in one form or another. This is why I don't believe in using magick in any negative fashion (aside from that fact that it just isn't nice).

I often use this rule as an example when I explain to nonPagans why there is no such thing as the wicked witch. "After all," I say, "if you magickally give someone warts, you are likely to end up getting hives in rude places. What self-respecting witch would risk that?"

In real life, following the Law of Returns is as simple as obeying the rule of Harm None. It can be hard to predict the exact results of your actions. And since witches believe that words and thoughts have power, the Law of Returns means that it is important to watch everything you say and think, in addition to what you actually do.

Impossible? Well, yes, it is. But that doesn't mean we shouldn't do our best. I have found that since I started to pay more attention to what I said out loud and what I thought to myself (for example: "I hate him" or "Man, that was stupid of me"), I have been much more aware of my own negativity and more apt to replace those negative thoughts and words with more positive ones. Have I seen a difference in what the universe gives back to me? You bet I have.

Which leads me to my third rule: Take Personal Responsibility.

Take Personal Responsibility

Witchcraft is a spiritual path of personal responsibility. We tend to believe that each person is responsible for his or her own actions, unlike some religions that blame the devil, or some sort of human predisposition toward sin, for a person's actions. It involves personal choice to deliberately harm another. And if you put negativity out into the universe and get crap back, that is your responsibility, too.

Don't get me wrong. I don't mean that we somehow did something to deserve every bad thing that happens to us. Bad things really do happen to good people. Sometimes there is a lesson to learn. Sometimes it may be part of a bigger plan that we human beings can't see. And let's face it, sometimes crap just happens. That's life.

On the other hand, many of life's ups and downs can be traced back to us. We choose how to respond to each situation. Choice is the important word here. This is where we get back to personal responsibility. You can't control everything that happens to you. But you can chose whether or not to respond positively and productively (like actively searching for a job once you've lost yours, and crafting some powerful prosperity magick to boost your chances of finding a new one) or negatively and unproductively (sitting in the corner, drinking and cursing out your significant other, your ex-boss, and whoever is in charge of the country at the time).

Why These Rules Are Important

I said at the beginning of this article that one of the great things about being a witch was that there weren't a lot of rules. But another aspect of Paganism that I love is that the rules we do have add up to one important concept: we have control over our own lives.

If you think about it, all three of these rules—Harm None, the Law of Returns, and Personal Responsibility—all mean that we can make a positive difference in our own lives, in the lives of others, and in the world around us. To me, that's what being a witch is all about.

Dallas Jennifer Cobb

In the Pagan community, there is amazing individuality and diversity. While this article acknowledges the vast differences among Pagans, it does not include practitioners of dark or harmful arts in its general observations of the Pagan community.

Though we are all unique in our particular Pagan identity, our commonly held beliefs reflect the underlying principles of our Pagan faith, and are woven through our rituals, practices, gatherings, and community. A few of our common beliefs are almost non-negotiable. For me, the three rules underlying my Pagan practice, the rules I live by, are:

- Harm no one

- What goes around comes around, and

- To my own self be true

These three rules encompass an evolved and complex thought system, developed over time, that helps to keep my words, attitudes, actions, and behavior under control. With the rules as a guide, I am able to live peacefully, fruitfully, and companionably with diverse communities; maintain a spiritual focus that reflects my deeply held beliefs; and actively engage in the creation of the kind of life I want to live—to be the kind of person I admire.

I wouldn't have a structure to keep me focused without rules to serve as a guidepost, and I might not truly thrive. Before you object to any imposition of rules, let me explain what they mean to me.

Harm No One

This rule underlies many practices and spiritual faiths throughout the world. Think of the Judeo-Christian Ten Commandments, the teachings of the Bible and the Qur'an. Even the Hippocratic oath that is taken by most doctors has the sentiment of "harm no one" imbedded within it. The Wiccan Rede supports the premise that harm no one is a universal Pagan belief: "Eight words the Wiccan Rede fulfill: An' it harm none, Do what ye will."

In my experience, most Pagans practice the notion of harming no one. Most practitioners of an earth-based and earth-honoring spirituality are guided by the cycles of Earth, Sun, and Moon. While we acknowledge the natural cycles of decay, composting, and rebirth, we do not subscribe to any destructive, harmful, or so-called "dark" arts. Universal laws, also sometimes called the Laws of Nature, do not change and cannot be broken. Universal law states that whatever you plant is what you will harvest.

Indeed, without such laws, our Pagan practice could be entirely different, succumbing to some of the so-called dark arts, engaging in destructive, oppressive, and undermining magic.

Most Pagans are aware of the dangers of planting harmful seeds. We know that when we plant a tomato seed, a tomato will grow. We have to ask ourselves—if we sow seeds of violence, hatred, intolerance, and corruption, what sort of crop will we harvest?

If you are observant of the cycles of nature, you know that the purpose of decay is to rot organic matter enough to create fertile soil. The growing of fruits, vegetables, trees, and flowers is the ultimate task of nature, and like the macrocosm of nature that we live

within, most Pagans want to grow goodness. So harm no one, plant only good seeds, and harvest a positive bounty. This leads to the second rule.

What Goes Around Comes Around

Universal law also holds that all energy is circular. So the concept of "what goes around comes around" has its roots in finite science. It is derived from physics, and the universal law that describes how energy moves. All energy molecules, atoms, and the planets move in a circular motion. Since we humans are made up of energy, this universal law applies to us and by extension to our interactions.

Universal laws exist in a wide variety of cultures and are included in many religious and spiritual texts. They are often heard as slogans, stated as rules, or used as catch-all phrases in response to many situations. They also appear in old adages and sayings. Tried and tested over time, these laws have helped to keep us on a path of helpful, uplifting, and prosperous living. Indeed, without such laws, our Pagan practice could be entirely different, succumbing to some of the so-called dark arts, engaging in destructive, oppressive, and undermining magic.

Let's face it. Life is hard, and there is lots of hurt in it. There are also lots of hurtful people. While I don't believe in hurting other people and go to great lengths to make sure I don't harm myself, there are times when I feel hurt by other people or situations. It is during those times that I face the deep spiritual challenge of trying not to succumb to the desire for revenge. It is sometimes easy to justify hurting someone else, because they hurt me first. But, I believe that what goes around comes around, and that means for every action there is an equal and opposite reaction.

When I am faced with a desire for revenge, I remind myself both of the universal law and the commonly-held Pagan Three-fold Law, which states that everything comes back to you three times.

I know that I am unwilling to purposefully bring negativity into my life, as life has enough little difficult moments as it is, so I choose not to send negative energy out into the universe.

While I sometimes think vengeful thoughts, I do not act upon them. I go back to the universal law and am assured that there is no need for revenge, as the universe will indeed give back to everyone exactly what they dished out. So whoever did me wrong, will get theirs without me getting involved.

Not only does it make me feel as though my hurt has been revenged, but it keeps me from doing something bad that would come back on me. And it counsels me to be very aware of my actions, because what I do will come back to me for sure and, in all likelihood, threefold.

To My Own Self Be True

While I limit my magic to helpful magic, I also strive to be true to myself. That means that even though I am trying not to harm anyone else, I must also be sure not to harm myself. I continuously examine my intentions, making sure I don't compromise my own beliefs just to please other people. I don't need to diminish my own self-worth just to get someone to like me. And I don't need to abandon what I believe and hold close to my heart so I will fit in, either.

In some ways Harm No One encompasses To My Own Self Be True, and includes the premise that I don't harm myself either. This means honoring and uplifting my spirit and self-esteem; it means continuing to do the work that is necessary to heal my spirit and bring peace to myself and my life. Taking care of me is the most important work I do, because when I am well and fit, I am better able to care for my family, community, and planet.

Rules to Thrive By

If we accept that we live in an interactive cosmos and that what goes around comes around, it is crucial not to send out negative energy (Harm No One), not even to ourselves (To My Own Self Be True), then we have some commonality within community. These rules can support how we live and what we hold as valuable.

But don't worry, we need not apply or interpret these rules identically either. Because we are diverse, our interpretation and practice of these three rules will differ, too. My personal Pagan practice doesn't include the imbibing of alcohol or drugs, not even in ritual, because I believe that these substances are harmful to me. Others imbibe and feel good doing so.

While I respect other people's right to sexual freedom, and I witness lots of interesting expressions of sexuality in community and at rituals and gatherings, I choose to remain monogamous with my partner, because I don't want to harm our relationship.

So be unique, but think about creating positive Pagan communities by subscribing to these three rules to live by. Decide how they can apply to your life, your Pagan practice, and your interactions within your community. These really are rules to thrive by.

Susan "Moonwriter" Pesznecker

As the Pagan community grows and evolves, we address many of the same obstacles faced for centuries by mainstream spiritual traditions. We struggle with issues of whether to organize, how far to extend our reach, and whether we should charge for our services. We consider new and better ways to share information and teach younglings and persons new to the path. And, unfortunately, we run into those who proselytize and insist that their way is the one and only, real, honest, true, bona fide, authoritative way—a way written in the books, blessed by the gods, foretold by the ancients, or passed on through the family.

Just the other day, I happened on a Web site for a Druid group that claimed to be the only authentic Druid order in the world and that any other so-called Druid organizations were only play-acting. Likewise, a couple of weeks before that, I interceded in an argument in which one Pagan insisted loudly to another Pagan that "if you didn't cast a circle and call the watchtowers, it wasn't a 'real' ritual." These kinds of discord always set my teeth on edge, because they sound just like the arguments among the mainstream faithful who too often claim—loudly—that it's their way or the highway. As far as I can see, this kind of approach only fosters divisiveness and ends up making people feel disillusioned, defensive, or just plain awful. Spiritual strife drives wedges between us, and it creates divisions instead of fostering shared understanding. These disagreements inevitably happen when one person decides his or her religion is "right."

My First Rule: There Is No One True Way

Allow me to explain by using myself as an example. As a Pagan, I believe in the eminent nature of the universe. I feel that the Divine is within me, and that I have only to look within myself to find it. It's in the hug I exchanged with my dear friend last week; it's in the soil I turned in my garden yesterday morning, and in the last ritual danced under the Full Moon. While these views are my own, I think most magickal people agree that life itself is a dance with the Divine, and that one's personal approach to spirituality finds each person embracing that sacred energy in his or her own way. Some of us do this through formalized ritual, prayer, divination, trance, spellwork, or apprenticeship in a defined order. Others embrace the divine through art, meditation, solitary practice, or even via an afternoon walk through the woods.

What is sent out returns; what is taken must be replaced; what is borrowed must be returned; what is emptied must be refilled.

If we each strive to feel that same life essence, strive to understand that same essential energy or force and to enfold our lives around a blossoming spirituality, how is it that anyone else can decide his or her way is better or more true than someone else's? Can we meet on common ground? Can we agree that the wealth of earthly spiritual traditions are different ways to frame one's approach to and connection with universal energy past, present, and future? The person who is Wiccan, Druid, faerie, Dianic, chaos mage, Jedi, or Satanist has a path as true and real as mine—provided it is tempered with ethics and a sense of responsibility. Which brings me to ...

My Second Rule: Do No Harm

Earth is a closed, finite system, and we share the ride with billions of fellow souls. What we do each day, magickal or mundane, affects each of our fellow Earth-riders. Every decision we make, every piece of energy sent out into the world, every word uttered, every action taken causes a ripple in the grand cosmic pool and impacts life here on Earth. Therefore, it's our responsibility to make sure that our actions don't cause either real-time or rebound harm to others.

In my own mundane life, I'm a mother, nurse/healer, college teacher, and an impassioned earth-sign. I tend an organic garden and try to live sustainably, while also treating my fellow humans and living creatures with compassion and a sense of humor. In all ways, I work to avoid harming the planet and everyone and everything on her. I temper my magickal workings with care and responsibility, and avoid actions that could harm another. I carry out works that enrich and strengthen my world. For me, this reflects a sense of communal responsibility, a way of ensuring my actions enrich the multiverse rather than weakening it.

My Third Rule: Give Back

Every action has an equal and opposite reaction, and those who work regularly with magick understand that to use energy is to create a shift or even a void. What is taken must be replaced—balanced. In keeping with that, I don't follow the traditional Rule of Three. I believe

more in the Rule of One and find truth in this simple, singular idea of balance. What is sent out returns, what is taken must be replaced, what is borrowed must be returned, and what is emptied must be refilled. Taken in the other direction, what is used carelessly, without permission or restoration, tips the cosmic scales and generates chaotic tensions and negative effects. These truths apply not just to magickal energy but also to ethical practices and relationships with other living creatures. Giving back is a matter of social and communal responsibility. Even for Pagans, who are known for working on "Pagan time" and bristling in the face of authority because they want to do their own thing sans external rules and boundaries, it takes a village—and intentional cooperation—to work good magick.

These three simple rules provide me with an ethical, interwoven approach to daily magickal life. Follow these guidelines and you'll sow harmony and growth rather than discord and destructiveness. Follow them and you'll approach your fellow humans with compassion and understanding rather than antagonism. Your positive actions will feed your soul, and your "village" will thank you.

Deborah Blake *is a Wiccan high priestess who has been leading her current group, Blue Moon Circle, for many years. She is the author of* Everyday Witch A to Z: An Amusing, Inspiring & Informative Guide to the Wonderful World of Witchcraft (Llewellyn, 2008), The Goddess is in the Details: Wisdom for the Everyday Witch (Llewellyn, 2009), *and* The Everyday Witch A to Z Spellbook (Llewellyn, 2010).

Dallas Jennifer Cobb *lives an enchanted life in a waterfront village in Canada. She loves family, gardens, fitness, and fabulous food, and when she is not running on country roads or wandering the beach, she is writing and daydreaming.*

Susan "Moonwriter" Pesznecker *has practiced Earth-based spirituality for three decades. In addition, she is a registered nurse, holds a master's degree in nonfiction writing, and currently teaches college English. Susan is the author of* Crafting Magick with Pen and Ink (Llewellyn, 2009) *and* Gargoyles (New Page, 2007); *her work has also appeared in several of the Llewellyn annuals and calendars. Sue is a practicing herbalist and teaches green magick, herbology, and healing at the online Grey School of Wizardry (www.greyschool.com).*

Illustrator: Tim Foley

Pen Pals and Prison Friends

Gail Wood

As with many important lessons, my Pagan prison correspondence service started by accident with good intentions and high hopes. Several years ago, before the ubiquity of Internet-based directories, the leader of our Pagan group put our addresses in a national Pagan directory, hoping that we would make contacts with Pagans in our area. What we got were letters from a few incarcerated Pagans, from different locations across the country. We added them to our mailing list and sent them our newsletter, which was full of articles and events.

As the editor of the newsletter, I received letters, too, and after the third or fourth one, I called my friend and left a message on her voice mail in which I sort of laughed about our "new friends." I guess we could call them "felon friends," I said, and the name stuck. From then on, we referred to our burgeoning prison correspondence as "the felon friends." There were less than half a dozen men writing to us, and we started writing letters in response to their inquiries.

Because our in-person circle drew people from a large geographic region, where winter weather was severe, we tried to offer some services through the mail. I began offering our circle's monthly dark moon ritual lesson through correspondence. The first year, a small

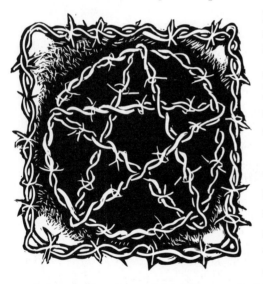

percentage of the students taking the course were incarcerated, but after the first year, nearly everyone taking the correspondence course was a prisoner.

The correspondence course was passive during the first years. I sent out chapters with lessons and a ritual, and it was up to the prisoners to complete the lessons and the rituals. Many of the prisoners faithfully reported on their progress and on their struggles on being Pagan in prison.

As I drifted away from the in-person group, the prisoners continued to write to me. Some would give me advice on how to deal with prisoners. They told me how to tell the difference between the sincere seeker and a manipulator or fake. They began passing my name on to other prisoners, and my correspondence courses grew.

The first course became a published book. Then, I started a second course on the male aspect of Pagan deity, a sort of "god of the month" club. This time, all the people taking the course were incarcerated. It was very absorbing work, and an act of service to a segment of our community that has long been hidden. The prisoners asked for more interaction, more direct comments on their work, assistance with their spiritual challenges, and feedback on their lessons. Later, I offered a tarot class. And for several years, I offered an intense beginning Wicca class that had chapter-by-chapter questions that required responses from the student and feedback from me.

In order to respond to these expectations, it became clear to me that I needed to be less casual and more organized. Many of these prisoners regarded me as their teacher and priestess and I felt the need to honor that. I also realized that this was a challenge from my gods and that I needed to "get real" and act like what I offered was a service and, in a very real sense, a ministry.

Learning the Rules and Hard Facts

As I began corresponding in earnest, I learned some hard facts about prisons. I had students in many different states, and the rules for receiving materials other than a one-ounce letter varied widely. In some states, prisons would not allow any letter or envelope that weighed more than one ounce; others required that religious materials be marked in some way; and still others required special permission for the prisoner to enroll in a correspondence course.

I was asked to credential myself as a priestess and teacher, which is difficult for Pagans since most of us are self-taught or ordained

through small unincorporated groups. Mailroom guards in some prisons would exercise personal judgments about the material received by inmates. More than once, the tarot course, in particular, was stopped by mailroom personnel even though it was approved by the prison or the state's Department of Corrections.

Prison rules for religious materials vary greatly across the different states. Some try to accommodate inmate spiritual learning while others are not accommodating. The rules for receiving letters and packages also vary according to the level of prison security. It may seem obvious that a medium-security prison would have less stringent rules than a maximum- or super-maximum-security prison, and sometimes I didn't find out until the materials were returned (often without an explanation). Sometimes, the materials were confiscated, and the prisoner had to deal with an extensive bureaucracy in order to get the lessons; other times, access was denied.

I learned a great deal about what spiritual life is like in prison. Most of the prisoners who wrote didn't disclose a lot of the harshness of their lives: about living without privacy or control over most aspects of their lives, or the presence of anger, boredom, violence, and danger. As I tried to teach them from a distance, I learned how many of my assumptions about the essentials of Pagan spiritual practices are not viable in prison.

Sometimes, Pagan practice can be oriented to having the right accoutrements. The freedom to have incense, salt, feathers, and other things was not always possible for prisoners; and there were the more obvious prohibitions against fire, candles, wands, and athames. This challenge stretched me to be more creative in my practice as I advised them on ways to have a dynamic spiritual life in the absence of the things I previously had thought were necessary. What I realized was that these things made spiritual practice easier, but their absence made it possible to strengthen the spirit by the creative exercise of the will and the spirit.

While those of us on the outside often bemoan the absence of community, most of us have access to books, materials, and Web-based information. Most of us are able to put together a solitary practice with the resources available. In prisons, access to information and physical items is severely limited. My challenge as a teacher was to develop authentic lessons that would help them in their spiritual practice as Pagans.

I developed a rigorous series of lessons called *The Initiation of Athena: Knowing the Craft.* The students were required to answer questions and send them back before they got the next lesson. The lessons were rigorous for the teacher as well, because I wrote comments on each one, answered other ancillary questions, and then mailed the comments and next lesson back to the prisoner.

I also developed a questionnaire (see below) to gauge their intentions and to eliminate the "lonely witch prisoner seeking pen pal" letters. These questions were designed to measure their commitment to spiritual learning and level of skill.

1. Describe your educational background and work life.

2. Describe your family situation, with attention to spiritual background and resources (or lack of) for support in your spiritual seeking.

3. Most people have a guide or rule that helps them make choices in difficult situations. Phrases such as "do no harm" and "do unto others as you would have them do unto you" are examples of these. Do you have such a phrase that you actively use as a measure for your difficult choices? If you do, please tell me what it is, and briefly what it means in terms of behavior and choices.

4. What is the role of spirituality in your life?

5. What would you like it to be?

6. Name a book that has influenced you and why.

When I asked them about the ethics, I wanted to know the guidelines that framed their lives and their thinking. Many wrote about the Wiccan Rede. A few others shared thoughtful insights into how it was to live dishonestly and then to live in the world of prison with its strict boundaries, rules, and shadow society of violence and anger. Here is one very eloquent reply:

"Honestly, I've tried to live by the eight words 'An it harm none, do as ye will,' but I am struggling with my criminal background.

The truth is that once I violated the will of others and was sent to prison for 50 years, I learned that I cannot live by the Rede in prison. It's virtually impossible to harm none when others live by completely opposite rules. Also—and I'm a little ashamed to admit this—despite the fact that I was caught and arrested, I'm a fairly successful criminal. I realize this is a horrible thing to say, but it's true. As of seven years ago, I've been focusing on building other skills, on focusing my criminal talents to positive uses. You ask me for a rule or guide that I can use? And do? I guess 'do what must be done to survive and keep the harm to a minimum.'

It's always been my belief that the Rede is not a strict law by which we must abide, but a guide for our moral choices and behavior.

Trying to Cope

As prisoners continued to pass my name along to other inmates and new students continued to write, the workload grew. What also became apparent was that Pagan prison ministry had limited financial resources and limited support from other Pagans. Mainstream denominations have the advantage with long-term, organized, and financially supported prison programs that include access to legal counsel and legal advice. In the Pagan world, prisoner support is usually done by small groups or individuals, and there is no financial or legal infrastructure.

I learned that working with prisoners is not well understood by people in the free world, nor do they particularly want to know about Pagans in prison. Most middle-class people, Pagan or not, have limited exposure to jails, prisons, and long-term incarceration. Even with this country's enormous growth rate in its prison populations, most people are comfortable in their assumptions that neither they nor their friends and family will ever live in a prison. With more than two million men and women in prisons and jails across the country, and with an annual growth rate of nearly 13 percent for state prisons, many of us will not be able make that assumption for very much longer. When I began to talk about the prison work I was doing, most people expressed a concern about prisoners who would seek me out and, by extension, seek them out, when they were released. Most people didn't want to be involved and many didn't want to hear about my work with prisoners.

Too Many Assumptions

When the number of prisoner-students taking my course grew to more than thirty, I did a small survey. The majority returned the survey, and I learned that some of my rather idealistic notions were wrong. I had a rather naïve assumption, for example, that most were incarcerated because of the harsh drug laws in this country. In fact, most of the prisoners taking my course were in prison because of violent crimes. I also learned that more than half had gotten their GED while in prison, and only a few had post-secondary educations. Most of them became Pagan after going to prison and learning about it by word of mouth or through reading a book. Most were financially destitute, meaning they could barely afford the money for stamps and small personal items. I heard a lot of stories about writing to many Pagan groups and hearing nothing in return. Less than 1 percent of my students were women throughout the seven years I taught correspondence courses. While services in male prisons are sparse, there are even fewer services for women prisoners.

I began to understand that most of my ideas about this accidental ministry were naïve. Most of the prisoners had lived lives of anger and violence, and, indeed, many had done some very bad things. Their world of imprisonment often demands that they continue to seek solutions based in anger and violence. It is stating the obvious

that prisons are bad places. While their true purpose is rehabilitation, prisons really are more about punishment and containment and not for promoting internal peace. Many prisoners, including a lot of the ones who were my students, chose to "do their time well," as they call it. Many tried to learn as much as they could and sought to understand themselves better in order to lead more successful lives.

Being successful in the free world after leaving prison is a big challenge, however. Having a strong spiritual life is no guarantee that someone will do well on the outside, either. The first time one of my students was sent back for violating his parole, I was surprised because he had really strong intentions and family support. His old ways of being and reacting were still deeply ingrained in him, though. After prisoners get out, most want to have nothing to do with their old prison life, including the things that helped them through it. Many of my students had good intentions to keep up with their studies, but none did. They had many demands and distractions after being released, and their main focus needed to be on maintaining a strong, successful life in their new freedom.

I accept occasional phone calls from inmates, all of whom must call collect. In my home state, the ministerial services for the Department of Corrections often call with questions about how to accommodate Pagan practice within its prisons. And sometimes a prisoner's demands for religious accommodation can be outrageous. As an advisor, the difficulty lies in finding a balance between what is necessary or desired and the stringent demands of prison rules. Also true is that Pagan spiritual practice is most often based on the individual and is not standardized, so what is true for me is not always true for other Pagans.

An inmate who had never been my student sued me, most of his facility's officers, and the chaplain, based on some advice I'd given to the chaplain who, in turn, had interpreted that advice.

One day, I discovered that an inmate had given my name and address to a newsletter serving incarcerated Pagans, stating that I offered free correspondence courses. My student numbers swelled to one hundred before, belatedly, good sense prevailed and I started turning people away. Up until that point, I had thought that this ministry was a disguised gift from the gods and I was supposed to accept the serious students. I learned, though, that the lesson was about my own ability to set boundaries and to be assertive about my own time and money.

Burnout Brought Necessary Changes

With so many indigent students spread across twenty-three states, I had to devote two hours every night and one weekend day every week to manage correspondence with the inmates, and that was in addition to my busy personal life and career. I also had a significant number of in-person students, all of whom needed time and attention. The prisoners continued to ask for more services, a newsletter, and more lessons. The copying, postage, and expenses continued to add up, as did their demands and criticism. It wasn't all negative, however. Many prisoners sent small, delightful gifts—drawings, stamps, and things they had made.

I am not proud of how I handled this out-of-control growth. I knew I was burnt out and overextended. I got so far behind in my correspondence that at one point, I took vacation days to catch up. Even then I wasn't able to finish.

After spending two evenings reading reproachful letters, I cut back the amount of time I spent reading letters. Then, after a week-long vacation with my family, I did not resume my demanding routine. I started to refuse phone calls from inmates. I had intended to go back to the faithful correspondents and apologize, to rework the course and make it smaller. However, one day, after a long-delayed visit to my post office box, I got a summons for a lawsuit.

An inmate who had never been my student sued me, most of his facility's officers, and the chaplain, based on some advice I'd given to the chaplain who, in turn, had interpreted that advice. Fortunately, the department of corrections designated me as a consultant, so I was represented by the state's attorney general's office. It took several months for the case against me to be dismissed. During that time, my intentions to resume my correspondence courses evaporated. Another attempt at a lawsuit followed that first one. While my involvement was quickly dismissed, it was dispiriting to know that the people I had tried to help were willing to take this kind of action. Their actions added to my discouragement.

There is a deep desire among seekers in prisons for our teaching, our rituals, and our concern—indeed, for our community. For those among us who choose this service, I have some practical advice.

- Start small and expand in small increments.

- Honor the prisoners as human beings but know the reality of what they might have done and may continue to do.

- Keep good records; you will be asked to remember details of their responses.

- Get a post office box and don't give out your home address.

- Only give out your phone number and e-mail if you wish to receive contact from prisoners and, sometimes, their families.

- Don't do favors or errands—such as deliver packages, buy things, or make phone calls to other people—for them.

- Keep your relationship with them focused on your teaching or priestessing work; reveal personal information about yourself only as it applies to these roles.

- Get training, if available, and seek the community of others offering similar services.

- Don't ask them what they did to get them in prison unless you really want to know; because as a priest or priestess, you will have to decide what crimes will lead you to refuse them aid.

- Know the rules of the facilities where the inmates are located; be honest and try not to make promises you can't keep.

- Say no firmly when you need to.

- Know yourself and know you will learn more about yourself in the process.

There are some large Pagan groups that may be good resources. Both the Circle and the Druid Network have strong infrastructures. Pagan Pastoral Outreach program in Ontario, Canada, has a resource-rich online site at www.ppo-canada.ca with links to some very helpful online discussion groups.

A Pagan prison ministry, whether through correspondence or in person, is absorbing, challenging, and rewarding work. My regrets center on my naiveté, lack of boundaries, and the ignoble ending of the work, not in the work itself. To be their teacher and priestess for a time was an incredible and humbling honor—a gift from the gods.

Gail Wood *is a witch, priestess, and teacher living near Ithaca, NY. She is the author of four books and numerous articles on Pagan topics. Her Web site is www.rowdygoddess.com, and she may be contacted by e-mail at darkmoonwitch@earthlink.net.*

Illustrator: Rik Olson

Chakra Balancing and Tarot
Calantirniel

When I did readings at a New Age bookshop years ago, I encountered a most unusual situation. A woman came to me for a tarot reading, and upon reading her cards, I thought it was one of the most favorable readings I had ever encountered. Love was coming, money was coming, and a time of great enjoyment was at hand. I was so happy to relay this good news to her, but when I did, something unexpected happened. She began to cry. Then she told me that for well over two years other readers had told her the same things and none of these things had happened.

I instantly knew that there were blockages around her that did not allow her to accept these incredible gifts. I did not have time to provide a long healing session, but I felt inspired to use the tarot cards to do a reading on her chakra system. The reading would troubleshoot the problems, as well as show how the problems started. It would also teach her how to balance and maintain her energies so that she could then accept and receive everything her readings had promised for so long. Later, I began to do this layout for other clients who experienced great success in their healing. Subsequently, they attracted more desirable opportunities in their lives.

Draw a Card for Each of the Seven Chakras

Very briefly, the chakras can be described as non-physical, energetic "wheels" inside of our bodies. It is in these energetic centers that certain vibrational levels of universal energy enter, are processed, and also are released from our bodies. All the chakra centers are supposed to work in a balanced and interrelated manner.

If there is a blockage, or other imbalance, in one or more chakras (usually caused by fear), the processed energies that are released can attract people, things, and events that can teach about the imbalance—often in stressful and unpleasant ways. When the energy block is corrected, more desirable results will then enter the sphere of experience.

While space in this article will not permit a complete description of all seventy-eight tarot cards, there are many resources that describe the energies of these cards. Then, knowing the energetic signature of the cards, you can use your creativity to apply their messages to the chakra system, which is described briefly here. Please note that there is some subtle disagreement between sources, so if in doubt, ask to be guided by spirit in your work.

CROWN CHAKRA (PURPLE/VIOLET): SELF-KNOWLEDGE

Located at the top of the head, the color can also be described as a bright golden, or white, light. We connect to God/Spirit, or the "All That Is," through this chakra that oversees the entire spiritual body, as well as the upper brain, the pituitary/pineal glands, and the nervous and endocrine systems. Imbalances can be reflected as a feeling of disconnection from the body, a highly religious lifestyle, or a rigid or overly mental approach to living (living in your head), while disregarding emotion or the true essence of spirit. Imbalance can also be experienced as physical dizziness, headaches, and even a head injury.

BROW CHAKRA (INDIGO): SELF-REFLECTION

Located in the third-eye area, from the middle of the brow bone to the back of the head in the space under the skull. This is where our psychic and intuitive abilities reside, including but not limited to clairvoyance, or spiritual sight. This can give us our inner knowing that doesn't need to be proven with so-called facts, and can be described as extrasensory. Physically, the Brow chakra is the domain of the eyes and lower brain, and it includes the pituitary/pineal glands. Imbalances often express themselves as an improper use of doubt, or an inability to trust what you know. Physical manifestations of imbalance in this chakra include vision problems, insomnia, and (like the Crown chakra) dizziness and headaches.

THROAT CHAKRA (BLUE): SELF-EXPRESSION

This chakra is connected to expression and communications; it is where we "speak our truth." It also assists hearing and the upper respiratory system. My favorite description for this chakra is as follows: if the universe is a bank account with an infinite balance, the

Throat chakra is the ATM card with which we make our withdrawals. Think about that—what we say becomes our reality. Recognizing this type of power takes great responsibility, and it needs to be fully embraced. Imbalances can be expressed as an inability to share your feelings through words (being afraid to speak your mind). Imbalance my appear on the physical level as thyroid issues, throat soreness, laryngitis, or coughing, or as a feeling in the throat closing that makes it difficult to talk or breathe. These can be caused by either not using your voice, or using your voice in an untruthful manner, both of which are caused by fear, not love.

Heart Chakra (Green): Self-Acceptance

The Heart chakra is the only chakra that cannot be overactive, which gives the saying "Open up your heart" an even deeper meaning. How can anyone love too much? If you think this is possible, please re-examine your beliefs and realize that it is more likely you love yourself (and perhaps others) too little! This is the chakra where empathy and compassion, as well as thankfulness and gratitude, get expressed. Imbalances in this chakra can appear as a belief in lack or limitations, poverty consciousness, stinginess, bitterness, a "me first" attitude, or expecting the world to do things

for you without first being thankful or opening up—basically, anything that withholds the natural flow of abundant, loving energy. Physically, this can be reflected as problems in the shoulders, lungs, thymus gland, and immune system, or heart or circulatory problems. Since heart disease is one of the leading causes of death in our culture, some special emphasis ought to be focused here, regardless of the reading. This chakra is also instrumental in balancing the others, as it interfaces the three upper spiritual chakras with the three lower mundane chakras.

SOLAR PLEXUS CHAKRA (YELLOW): SELF-DEFINITION

Located beneath the small of the ribcage at stomach level, this very interesting chakra is where we experience "separateness" (ego) as we live in our bodies on the physical plane. This is the place we learn to shine (like the Sun) as individuals and to experience self-worth. This is also the first place I look for unhealthy attachments that are not based on our highest good. It is tricky to find a healthy, balanced place between our personal power and our connection to the All That Is; and the survival mechanism present in this chakra (as well as the Sacral and Root chakras) can be overwhelming. Because of this, we often succumb to fear and anger (expressed or not) through this chakra. This can cause us to either minimize ourselves (give away our power, allow others to take from us without putting our foot down, do things for others but not for ourselves, etc.) or maximize ourselves by being demanding or pushy, taking things before others can even if we don't need them, and inflicting our will without due consideration. In order to locate the fine point of self versus other(s), it is necessary to eliminate fear, to receive and integrate love, to express our true selves, and to acknowledge our intuition and spiritual connection and see things beyond the way they appear in the mundane. On a physical level, the Solar Plexus chakra relates with the upper digestive system, including but not limited to the spleen, stomach, pancreas, liver, and gall bladder.

Sacral Chakra (Orange): Self-Gratification

Also known as the chakra where we experience nourishment and nurturing, the Sacral chakra is located approximately three inches below the belly button. It can be referred to by what Hindus would nickname the "Money Pot," due to its role in creation and manifestation, which takes expression in the Throat chakra. Due to its lunar, watery nature, the Sacral chakra resonates with our emotional stability, pleasure, and sexuality; and, physically, with the kidneys/bladder, the lymphatic and lower digestive systems, as well as our reproductive organs. Addressing problems with these areas (a common expression for women is yeast imbalance) is to learn how to recognize and fulfill, and not to deny, our own needs before attempting to fulfill others' needs. Also, drink lots of good water and other healthy fluids.

Root Chakra (Red): Self-Preservation

Whereas the Crown chakra is our connection to spirit and pure consciousness, the Root chakra is our grounding root into our material existence on Earth. It relates to survival instinct, the adrenal fight-or-flight syndrome, and trust in one's ability to create material stability and foundations. It also relates to our physical body needs through the excretory systems, pelvis, and even our legs and feet. Problems with this chakra include bone-alignment issues, low-back pain, sciatica, scoliosis, hemorrhoids, constipation, lower-extremity problems, heat/cold issues, a feeling of being ungrounded, and financial difficulties. Also, in severe cases of neglect, abuse, or other survival issues, this chakra often needs work. Trust in the support of the universe needs to be learned and then translated into the physical.

To Do a Reading

Shuffle the tarot deck at least three times, and have the client cut the deck in the usual manner. Then, deal the top seven cards, with card one representing the Crown. Place the remaining cards in a vertical row down to Root chakra. Or if you prefer, you can place the first card at the Root chakra and work up to the Crown chakra. Use the method that feels right to you. One reader I know is very familiar with chakras, and she deals the Heart chakra first, then the higher chakras, and finishes with the lower ones. Experiment and use the method that works best for you. If doubts arise, you can use clarification cards in the usual manner for accessing a deeper understanding of the chakra in question.

If a chakra is closed or underactive, recommend the use of the chakra's color, either in the person's clothing or environment. Have them use crystals and even eat foods of the color needed, while holding the intention to open the blocked chakra. If a chakra is found to be overactive, it may be compensating for an underactive chakra, and it will likely balance out. While not necessary, dowsing with a pendulum as well as having a working knowledge of energetic healing modalities, such as Reiki, crystals, flower essences, and the Emotional Freedom Technique (EFT) can provide the next steps after this layout is assessed. Again, resources can be easily located, and many are available at no cost online. If you are a tarot reader or doing some other type of psychic/divinatory work, I recommend integrating healing into your practice, as healing will greatly empowers your clients. And you cannot help but receive some healing for yourself in the process. How can you lose?

SAMPLE READINGS

A sample reading for a woman is as follows:

Crown: King of Cups
Brow: Nine of Swords (reversed)
Throat: Queen of Swords
Heart: Queen of Disks (reversed)
Solar: The World (reversed)
Sacral: Ace of Disks (reversed)
Root: The Devil

At first glance, we can see she has good spiritual relations, and expresses herself well with articulate authority. However, we see some adjustments need to be made with the energies in her heart and lower chakras. The fact that the Queen, the Ace of Disks, and the World card show themselves in reverse says she has the ability to manifest financial prosperity, but it is blocked. Further searching will reveal the core issue. In this case, it is the Root chakra and the Devil card that represent fear, as well as the flesh/material plane. This was verified in that she was raised by a good father who was religious, but she needed to find her connection with Spirit, and did so. Now, she is attempting to leave behind work that meant a steady paycheck but was utterly life-sucking to her soul and her life force. She knew what she wanted to do, but was worried and afraid to leave behind the steady paycheck. I realized that when cards are reversed, it is just an imbalance in energy that is already there. Rather than working with color, I decided to work with her to turn the energies she already had around. We addressed the Brow chakra issue so she would trust her intuition instead of needlessly worrying.

I felt like the Queen of Swords in his Heart chakra was an ex-girlfriend he was trying to get over, to which he agreed.

Then, with the Root chakra, we needed her to feel connected not to the job, but to the Source—then she needed to trust that the Source was there and when she refined and then expressed her desires (Throat), the Source would unfold events that would bring perfect situations for her (Sacral and Solar). In order to receive these new situations, with our open Heart chakra, we need to say thank you, as if we have already encountered what is desired, then release it to the wisdom of the Source to bring it to manifestation. This is the key that sets everything in motion, so clarify and express your intention by saying thank you. Then, release it to the universe and trust that it will arrive at the perfect time and in the perfect way. Also know that if it isn't perfect, we can still be thankful and send it back out with our refinement of intention to receive something even better. I later learned she received a wonderful job offer for doing exactly what lifted her heart, and when we love our job, the money surely follows!

Here is another example; this one is for a man:

Crown: Justice
Brow: 9 of Wands
Throat: Queen of Cups (reversed)
Heart: Queen of Swords (reversed)
Solar: The Chariot
Sacral: Three of Swords
Root: King of Wands (reversed)

The chakras working here are the Crown, Brow, and Solar. This is very good, as it tells me this person is connected to Spirit, has good intuition, and follows it, because his gut will agree with his head, and he knows how to receive. I felt like the Queen of Swords in his Heart chakra was an ex-girlfriend he was trying to get over, to which he agreed. His Root chakra was showing me that he felt a bit emasculated, and he agreed, saying he wished to be the main material provider in a relationship. So the idea was to correct his attracting "imprint" so that he attracted the type of relationship he wanted, and also to be able to forgive himself and release his ex more fully. I saw a connection between the Throat and the Sacral, and asked him about his mother. Sure enough, she was a fairly self-indulgent lady who didn't nurture her kids enough, particularly him. He also felt that he was never really heard by her. So, upon acknowledging the source of this pattern, I needed to show him that he deserved nurturing, and that he needed to learn how to nurture himself (work with orange, even orange foods), and to feel he could express his truth (work with blue also). This, in turn, helped him to release his ex from his heart and feel like a strong man (fixed the Root). In a short time, he was dating a lady who was much kinder to him, very receptive and giving, and really listened to what he said!

May this technique enrich your tarot readings and provide deep healing for you and others!

RESOURCES

Greer, Mary K. *Greer's 21 Ways to Read a Tarot Card*. Woodbury, MN: Llewellyn, 2006.

Johari, Harish. *Chakras—Energy Centers of Transformation* (Revised and Expanded). Rochester, VT: Destiny Books/Inner Traditions, 2000.

Mumford, Jonn. *A Chakra & Kundalini Workbook: Psycho-Spiritual Techniques for Health, Rejuvenation, Psychic Powers and Spiritual Realization*. St. Paul: MN: Llewellyn, 2002.

Porter, Tracy. *The Tarot Companion, An Essential Reference Guide*. St. Paul, MN: Llewellyn, 2000.

INTERNET RESOURCES

Free Emotional Freedom Technique (EFT) Manual: www.emofree.com

Free Flower Essence e-Books: www.edwardbach.org

James Deacon's free Reiki e-Books: www.aetw.org

Solarraven/Peggy Jentoft's informative Web site: www.pjentoft.com

Calantirniel *became a certified Master Herbalist in 2007. She lives in western Montana with her husband and daugher, while her son is off at college. She also manages to have an organic garden and crochets professionally. Find out more about Calantirniel at www.myspace.com/aartiana.*

Illustrator: Kathleen Edwards

Pagan Charity:
Do We Practice It?

Magenta Griffith

Paganism and witchcraft are, by their very nature, run almost entirely by volunteers. We are our own priestesses and priests. We usually meet in each other's homes. We don't have much in the way of buildings and facilities, and our teachers and clergy need to have "day jobs" for the most part. This means we do what we do for love, but it can lead to a cavalier attitude toward the importance of our own spirituality, uneven support for our leaders and institutions, and, in too many cases, burnout.

How do we pay for our Paganism, our witchcraft? For British traditional witches, the laws of the Craft state that no charges for teaching or initiations can be levied. There are no other specifics on how we apply our money and our time to our spirituality. Many teachers will ask for money to cover the cost of space and supplies, but few are compensated for their effort. We don't make our livings as professional Pagans or witches; hence the witticism that the difference between Paganism and the New Age is the number of figures after the dollar sign.

We tend to rely on the Witch's Rede as our ethical guideline: "An It Harm None, Do What Thou Wilt." This is fine for telling us what not to do. It does not tell us what we should do. In many ways, this is a good thing. Our principles call for us to figure it out for ourselves, in our own situations. But it can mean that we look out for ourselves and those close to us and pay less attention to the larger good.

How do we determine what actions we should take in light of the Rede? In a given situation, is there anything that we should do or need to do to prevent harm? Most of us agree that we should support causes greater than ourselves with our time and money whenever possible. But how much money should we give, and how much time should we spend on our Pagan activities? There is no shared Pagan vision of charity that we can use as a guide regarding who to give money to, how much to give, and why. There is no common virtue of visiting the sick, the shut-in, of helping the elders among us. There are many activities present in conventional religions that are missing among us. Some of this we see as a good thing; there is no one to tell us what to believe, or who tries to part us from large sums of money. But because we have no guidelines on what we should do, we may find that the Pagan sick are alone, the Pagan elderly are neglected, and many Pagan organizations fail or stumble along year to year and never quite make ends meet.

Mainstream religions usually have a core set of beliefs, values, and writings that are central to those who follow that faith. Pagans and witches generally do not. We have no central authority, and no one sacred text. A friend of mine likes to say that Pagans are not the people of the book, they are the people of the library. We look to many sources for wisdom. But because of this, we may come to vastly different conclusions about how to act. We agree on the Wiccan Rede, we are inspired by the Charge of the Goddess, but we don't have any clear instructions on "how to be a good Pagan." We have no general rules for how to treat other people except Harm None.

One difficulty is the diversity among Pagans and witches. We often get our ideas about charity from the religions we grew up in, and most of us didn't grow up with our current spiritual tradition.

So we may have very different ideas about what actions to take even within the same coven or grove. Some of the confusion comes from our rejection of more conventional religions. There are Pagans who think that because they grew up in churches that asked for money and they have rejected those churches, they must also reject the idea of giving money to any religious organization.

We also have a wide range of ideas about wealth and poverty and the community's role in helping the needy. Sometimes, our priorities help us make decisions about whether to give and where to put our time and money. Recently, a local Pagan suggested that people should cut back or eliminate their cable TV and contribute the difference to a local Pagan project. I don't see it in these terms. People are going to find the money to give, one way or another, or they won't.

Many people do need to set better financial priorities, but if cable TV is your main form of entertainment and news, and having it actually saves money because less money is spent for other forms of amusement, it is an simplistic suggestion. And those expensive

The phrase "Thou Art God, Thou Art Goddess" came from the Church of All Worlds, who got it from the novel *Stranger in a Strange Land* by Robert Heinlein. Heinlein found that concept, which has been adopted by many Pagan groups, in Hinduism.

lattes that some of us buy may seem like a mindless habit, but what if it is your way to contribute to the owner, who is an old high school friend? We all have to make financial choices. Even the poorest among us find ways to contribute our pennies to causes we consider important. Furthermore, the well-to-do can always find excuses not to contribute, no matter how great the need.

Where we spend our money and our time is an indication of our true priorities. If we spend money on the latest toys and gadgets, but not on or in our Pagan community, what does that say about our commitment to our spiritual path? If we show up when it's time for a ritual and expect other people to do all the work, why are we surprised when covens explode and organizations fail? Where is our time and money going and what else could we do with it?

Most of us are not starving or living in hovels. We can exercise choices about contributing to a local, national, and international cause that is aligned with our beliefs, or support political candidates who support our values. We also need to pay our bills, feed our children, and put away something for our retirement years. So, how do we balance our personal needs and the needs of the larger group? We have to decide for ourselves and make our own choices. But consider this: if we can neglect others, are we abiding by the law of Harm None?

When the witchcraft movement first started, it was composed primarily of small groups of people in covens, often working with little contact with others. Today, Pagan groups are better organized, and the social dynamic has changed. New concepts have came into circulation, and communication between groups has improved. The phrase "Thou Art God, Thou Art Goddess" came from the Church of All Worlds, who got it from the novel *Stranger in a Strange Land* by Robert Heinlein. Heinlein found that concept, which has been adopted by many Pagan groups, in Hinduism.

The explicit divinity of all people changed the social dynamic. From not knowing too much about others in your coven, lest they be compromised and betrayed, there was a gradual shift toward covens being a chosen family. So the relationships of people in the Craft and Paganism have changed over the years; they have become both

wider and more significant. Larger organizations and festivals that tend to draw people from many places have added to this trend.

Pagans have become more concerned for the environment and the natural world. If we believe that everything shares a spark of divinity, this must change who we care about—not just those physically and emotionally close to us, but all humans are our family. Not only that, but all animals, plants, and the Earth are our relations.

We tend to see our deities as working through us, rather than above or outside us. Therefore, we must do the work of the gods or it won't get done. Our actions are important. Harm None does not just mean refraining from action, but acting directly to prevent harm. On the other hand, we do not want to become self-righteous busybodies, convinced we know what actions are right, and condemning those who act differently from us.

We walk a fine line when determining what actions to take and what not to take. We need to make an ongoing examination of the resources, sharing, and tasks that our spiritual paths call us to perform. Paganism has become a tribal phenomenon, but people who act as if they have no community don't have community! Charity isn't just about giving money; it's also about taking care of kids and helping each other in whatever ways seem appropriate. What we give to the community comes back to us.

Your spirituality is not just about you and your relationship to your deity or deities; it's also about your relationship to your community and the rest of the world. No part of the natural world is isolated from the whole; this is the way Nature works. What each of us does with our money and our time is the real indication of what our true values are.

The Law of Threefold Return implies that whatever you do comes back to you threefold. That is not a strictly numeric principle; it's also a metaphor for karma. Every action contains potential consequences for ourselves and others. If we don't have some sense of communal responsibility, what kind of community have we created?

Magenta Griffith *has been a witch for more than thirty years and a high priestess for more than twenty years. She a founding member of the coven Prodea, which has been celebrating rituals since 1980, as well as a member of various Pagan organizations. She presents classes and workshops at a variety of events around the Midwest. Magenta shares her home with a small black cat and a large collection of books.*

Illustrator: Neil Brigham

Pagans and Prosperity Consciousness

Calantirniel

Nearly all humans—Pagan and non-Pagan alike—have prosperity and abundance issues. However, because Pagans embrace unconventional beliefs, practices, and lifestyles that others may find difficult to understand, the usual ways that non-Pagans tackle prosperity issues can be irrelevant to Pagans. Often, mainstream methods do not work for Pagans, so what can we do?

Many Pagans are conscious of energies and, indeed, do their best to live their lives in accordance with their beliefs, one of which is that our planet is alive and takes care of all of us, and that we are the stewards who need to nurture our planet as well as ourselves. Simply put, most Pagans lovingly seek the natural balance of things, seen and unseen, and experience spiritual connection this way. Many Pagans also come from upbringings that are not supportive of their belief systems and practices, or their lifestyle choices. Many are still attempting to figure out who they are because of this general lack of support. But, unfortunately, it is necessary to know ourselves before we can evaluate our relationships with material resources—prosperity, abundance, and wealth.

Prosperity, Abundance, and Wealth

To define prosperity, abundance, and wealth, we need to understand what we value. Rather than equating "value" to "having the most," I recommend a system that measures comfort, security, and freedom. If we can learn to maintain a balance between these, we can begin to tackle prosperity issues.

It is up to the individual, group, or family to determine where that balance is. A good way to determine the balance of comfort, security, and freedom is to gauge the pleasure received and compare it to the of amount of pain felt. The threshold between what constitutes pleasure and pain will be different for everyone.

Health is also worthy of consideration in this discussion of prosperity and abundance. Health can be examined on the physical plane, as well as the emotional, mental, and spiritual planes. After all, the energy of health is more crucial than the energy of money ever was. Having one's health also provides comfort and freedom.

To return to the material side of prosperity, however, there are two sides of the coin to consider. They are: obtaining resources and making money versus maintaining resources and spending money. On the making-money side, the idea is to do something that is truly of service to the world that you absolutely love doing for which fair compensation is received. Ideally, these services can be offered with minimal time and expense in order that compensation will not only cover costs of maintenance (the second side of the coin) but will go beyond that.

Trimming Expenses

Looked at from another perspective, the same gauge can be used to measure the value of things that are in your life. Do they provide you comfort or freedom? Do you want more comfort or more freedom? If you review your things and realize that some things are not providing either comfort or security (i.e., you own something only to impress people), or you are seeking one and not the other, it is time to get rid of those things. Either sell, give away, or throw away what does not provide comfort, security, or freedom, and make room for what it is you wish for.

For example, if someone wants to be free to travel and realizes the only reason they continue to work at a full-time job they don't like is to live in an expensive apartment, making different choices would make travel possible. Things in the apartment can be sold or given away, which would make it possible to live in a smaller space that cost less to rent. Lower rent could be paid for with the money from a part-time job or seasonal work, which would leave more time for travel. The tradeoff of less comfort for more freedom may be worthwhile.

I read about a couple who saved for a house by living in the woods on private property in a tent. They used technology while they were at work, and a cell phone while away from work. They figured out a way to eat well for less money. After a couple years, they were almost at their goal to pay cash and not have a mortgage payment. This is an example of prosperity consciousness—they loved living in the woods, and despite the hardships, they did not feel like they were doing without.

LIVING WELL WITHIN MEANS

Costs should not exceed the ability to pay (available resources). More expenses frequently means less freedom. And while more stuff can also mean more comfort, is the loss of freedom worth the comfort?

Remember the axiom "As above, so below." Well, it isn't better "up there" and crappy "down here." One is a mirror of the other. It is our responsibility to fix our problems. We need to "own our stuff," and not just our material stuff. We need to own our thoughts, beliefs, and actions as well. You will know it is "fixed" when the physical is manifested in the desired way without feeling you had to compromise your soul. This is obviously difficult to do, as we do not have many examples of this to learn from. Nearly all people live in the physical only, and those who are spiritual often spend their time and concentration only in the ethereal. The idea is to be utterly present in both the physical and the spiritual at the same time, not to go back and forth between one and the other. Keep working at it; this requires much coordination, but you will get there!

Common Expressions of Poverty Consciousness

Subconscious messages of not feeling deserving and worthy of receiving are often in our upbringing, and we don't always know what those beliefs are. For some people, poverty consciousness is born in the idea that we cannot like our work and follow our hearts at the same time. In other words, it is okay to do unfulfilling work if the earnings pay for security and things.

As an example, although a person may be drawn to art, music, drama, fashion, or some other creative field, family members say they will never make enough money (to buy security and comfort) in these careers. If, instead, the would-be artist learns to "play it safe" by becoming a doctor, lawyer, or computer engineer, life will be better. Beliefs such as these not only kill one's soul, they actually manifest poverty consciousness. In our fast-paced society, it has become more desirable to be a consumer, rather than a creator. It is easy to see how thoughts like these can disrupt the natural balance of things. I cannot think of one self-made, wealthy, abundant person who is not also creative and passionate about their work creation(s).

Some of us have poverty consciousness because our DNA carries an imprint of the collective experiences of all the hardships endured by our ancestors, many of whom endured some of the most difficult times on our planet. Many of those survival-type messages are very active in the subconscious, which is the basis of where we make our conscious decisions. Some of us have poverty consciousness through soul contracts in the past. As an example, I have heard of many spiritual workers and healers who are living today who had similar positions in past lives (many were monks, nuns, and the like). In those lifetimes, they had contracts (voluntary or involuntary) to provide their services without reciprocity, because, supposedly, "God and spirituality are free."

We need to remember that others, including many non-Pagans, really do value the same things we value.

Many of us have decided not to work for or take money from places that engage in beliefs and practices that are against our own values. These values mostly align with caring for our planet, and making choices that cause the least impact possible. We have also noticed that the largest proportion of high-paying positions, which are the easiest to obtain, do engage in activities that cause unnecessary damage to the Earth; that is unethical. The trick is to realize there is unlimited opportunity in whatever you truly wish to do. When you are aligned properly, many of the right opportunities will simply fall in your lap, and you can choose! We need to remember that others, including many non-Pagans, really do value the same things we value. This alone confirms that someone needs to provide these services or products—why can't it be you?

Making Changes through New Choices

I could give a long laundry list of things to do. After all, changing your entire vibration is not easy, especially when a person or group has so many decisions to make. Instead, I will help you maintain higher vibrational energy by providing a detailed meditation that you can repeat daily (same time of day or evening is best) for at least one Moon cycle (two cycles is even better), because this new energy of prosperity, abundance, and wealth needs to be thoroughly visualized and "felt." It also becomes a habit, and when it does, decisions become obvious and everything else falls into place.

MEDITATION

Call your spiritual work circle in whatever way you wish to do. The goal is love and healing for you and for all who surround you, and your intention for this work should be for the highest good. It is a great idea to at least light a candle to allow the feeling of sacred space around you. Ground yourself in Earth's energy by imagining your feet, or root chakra, becoming the roots of a tree. When your roots feel supported in the Earth, raise your arms overhead, like branches, reaching to the sky and spiritual contact from above. Imagine the Sun overhead warming you, and the the earth providing nourishing water to quench your thirst. Breathe deeply and really be in the present and in this space; feel all of your chakras, or spiritual vortices, opening and balancing in this energy. Know you are the center of the universe. Now, embrace more fully your innate, creative, abundant powers.

Imagine that you have magic scissors; see yourself cutting away any inappropriate cords that may be attached to you. Send them back to their source. If you can see these, they will look old, dark, murky, or even sticky. If you cannot see them, just know with all of your conviction that you are cutting the proper cords. See yourself surrounded by a Teflon-type shield so that these cords cannot reattach; and if they try to reattach, watch them slide off and cauterize themselves. Do not underestimate this work; it can cut away many lifetimes and generations of negativity. If you notice any cords are not releasing you, ask your guardian deity, or even the light of Christ consciousness if you align with that, to show you how to be free.

Now, it is time to call back to you any of your soul pieces that are ready to come back to help you create your "whole self." Some people have immediate recall of memories that they forgot, and this is a sure sign of this process working. In any case, know that you are becoming more complete and that you will in time integrate all of your energies into one strong energy.

It is now time to say, at least three times with as much meaning as possible:

I am giving and receiving in perfect balance, and I now accept and embrace all that the universe has to offer.

See your Solar Plexus chakra (below the joining of your ribcage) turn into a large glowing sun. Watch it grow as large as the room, even the city! See your Heart chakra swirling with bright pink and emerald-green light until it overflows. Intend balance and natural flow with the other chakras. See yourself awash with new ideas, creativity, and most of all, with love. When you can love yourself, you will be able to love others.

Re-do your "soul contract" by visualizing it and adding an addendum, such as:

I now wish to fully release all past soul contracts, and change all of the portions of my present soul contracts to forgive myself, forgive all others, and release all pain and struggle in all forms; and to allow health, ease, and abundance in all expressions into my life on all levels. It is done.

If you wish, write it out, sign your name, and date it—and make sure you mean it!

Imagine your guides showing you two fabrics of your life—one that is woven in strength and continuing, and one that needs to be unraveled down to the last thread—trust this process. Begin unraveling and see the patterns that need to be ended because they don't work anymore (at least be open to impressions). After the entire un-raveling-fabric disappears, see your current fabric "change" before your eyes into finer fabric. Watch it continue to weave itself in the new pattern. Really feel this process and observe what is leaving and what you are reclaiming! Allow yourself to investigate your place and your loving purpose in the world. Allow yourself to receive due compensation for your creative gifts.

Things from childhood may resurface to guide you to your true space, and to allow the outer world to bring guidance in whatever ways it will. See all of the work you have done radiating outward in all directions to your family, your friends, your work, and all who are in your energy. If they wish for abundance, they will still be in your energy. If they are not ready to release all they fear, they will leave your energy—be in awe at how Spirit accomplishes this. Children automatically receive these benefits, so if your goal is their healing, then heal yourself first, because that is the only way to truly help them.

When you are done, see yourself drawing in your branches, then drawing in your roots. Close your circle in your normal practice, and ground yourself with bread and beverage, or a bit of salt on your tongue. If you can, keep a journal for keeping track of feelings, events (ritual and mundane), symbols you notice, and accomplishments.

As you integrate the energies of your ritual work, things in your mundane, physical environment are going to change—they must in order to create what you want. Know many things (and perhaps people) need to leave your energy to make room for the vibration of prosperity and abundance that you wish to be in.

You may soon see how people truly buy into poverty consciousness. Trust that as you let these things go, new energies will replace what has gone with things and with people who match, more closely, your new energy vibration. No matter how uncomfortable it may get, keep making changes by making better decisions. Soon enough, the "bumpy exit" of old things and outworn relationships will begin to be replaced in surprising and wonderful ways. Accept and embrace these exciting changes with all of your being! May your road to prosperity be an uplifting one!

Calantirniel's *bio appears on page 113.*

Illustrator: Tim Foley

Become an Everyday Witch in 6 Easy Steps

Deborah Blake

There is no one "right" way to be a Pagan, witch, or Wiccan, or one "right" way to practice witchcraft. We each strive to find the path that suits us best. Some folks are content to celebrate the Full Moons and the sabbats, and live the rest of their lives more or less like everyone else. But for some witches, there comes a time when this is not enough. This moment may occur when they first discover the call of Paganism, or after years of walking the path of the witch. But no matter how it happens, or when, many of us reach a place where we say, "I want more." We

want to live our Pagan beliefs all day, every day, and integrate them into our day-to-day existence. I call this being an "everyday witch."

But how do you become an "everyday witch"? For most of us, the day is already full to bursting with obligations, work, and the never-ending To Do list. How can we possibly add in something else, no matter how important that thing might be?

On the other hand, how can we not?

After all, it is as important to feed the soul as it is to feed the body; and for many of us, walking the path of the witch is at least a part of what keeps us going, day after day. Not to mention that the tools and gifts of witchcraft can often be used to make our lives better—happier, healthier, and more prosperous—if we can just figure out a way to use them on a regular basis.

So here are six easy steps that will help you along the way to becoming an "everyday witch." You can use all of them or just one or two, whichever suits your needs and lifestyle best.

Step One: Create a Personal Practice

My practice of witchcraft changed the day I read Dianne Sylvan's wonderful book *The Circle Within: Creating a Wiccan Spiritual Tradition*. One of the chapters centered around building a daily practice, which Sylvan called "devotional rituals." By this, she meant simple rituals in which you connect with the deities, the God or Goddess, or both.

I sat down and thought about what I could realistically expect myself to do every day, even when I was tired or distracted or out of sorts, because, like everyone else, I have few perfect days. Initially, I couldn't come up with a ritual that was short enough, or simple enough, to fit these parameters. For a while, I tried standing at my altar every night, lighting a candle and saying a spell or a prayer, but some nights even that seemed like too much.

Then, I realized that I was using the word "ritual" too literally. After all, the important thing was to communicate with the gods, and to be open to the possibility of them communicating back. Looking at it that way, I saw that the solution was simple.

Now, I start each day by speaking to the gods. Before I get out of bed—often before I even open my eyes—I say out loud my morning greeting, which usually goes something like this: "Great Goddess, great God, I greet you at the start of another day and ask that you send me the best day possible. Help me to feel my best, so I might do my best for myself and for others."

I usually go on to ask for help with specific issues that concern me in the day ahead. I ask for protection for myself and those I love and close with "so mote it be." Then, I get up and go on with my day.

In the evening, after I have turned out the lights and closed my eyes, I end the day by talking to the deities again. But this time, instead of asking for help, I say thank you for all the good things that happened to me during the course of the day. This serves two purposes. I communicate my gratitude, but it also forces me to really think about the positive aspects of my life, even if they were as small as a good parking spot or a kind word from a friend.

These acts are simple and take very little time and energy, yet they make me feel more connected to my gods than I did before I started talking to them every day.

Your daily practice can be as simple as mine is, or as complicated as a full-out ritual that is complete with incense, garb, and drumming. What's important is not what you choose to do, but that you choose to do it at all. So figure out what you can reasonably expect yourself to fit into your schedule just about every day and find a way to reach out to whichever deity you believe in.

Step Two: See the Divine in the Mundane World

Witches believe that the divine is in everything. Each rock, each creature, each growing plant, and each of us contains a tiny spark of deity; a reflection of the greater divine that surrounds us. This belief is part of what makes magick work. We tap into that tiny bit of power in the crystal or herbs we use for our spells, and with it connect to the greater powers of the universe around us.

But when we're not working a spell, it can be easy to forget that magick is around us all the time, everywhere we go. So part of becoming an everyday witch involves paying more attention to the world we live in.

As I sit here typing into my laptop (which, let's face it, is kind of magickal all by itself), I can hear the song of the birds out my window. One of my cats, Samhain, is curled up against my leg. The wind blows through the screen to cool me, and the night is settling in, bringing calm and quiet. All magick. All blessed.

As you walk through your day, try to pay more attention to the little things that speak to you in tiny acts of magick. These don't

have to be anything spectacular: a child's laugh, the sound of water against a shore, a flower growing where no flower grew before—all these things are gifts from the gods. And be aware of so-called "co-incidences" that bring you just what you wished for, right when you wished for it. I find that the more I am conscious of these things happening, the more often they occur. For example, you need a new outfit to wear for a special occasion, and you walk by the window of a store and see the perfect one . . . and it's on sale! Other folks might ignore the little daily blessings and gifts that surround them, or take them for granted, but as witches, it behooves us to practice being more aware and more thankful for all that is divine and crosses our path as we walk through our daily lives.

Step Three: Turn Chores into Magick

Okay, let's face it—nobody *likes* doing housework. Yes, there can be a certain satisfaction in taking a messy space and turning it into a neat one, but most of us would rather read a book or watch television than mop the floor.

On the other hand, we all have to do it from time to time; it's a part of daily life. So why not add an element of magick, and make your chores a part of your witchy practice?

There are a number of ways to do this. The simplest is to add the element of "intent" to your housework. Much of the power of any magickal working comes from our focus and intent as we set out to achieve our purpose, whatever it is. For instance, if you are doing work for prosperity, you may start by visualizing yourself earning more money or receiving good news of a financial nature.

With each sweep of the broom, visualize yourself whisking away any negative energy left by bad news, arguments, or visitors with less-than-positive vibes.

Therefore, if you want to add a witchy element to your mundane cleaning chores, you can take a moment before you start to focus on your intent to cleanse your home not only on a physical level, but also energetically. With each sweep of the broom, visualize yourself whisking away any negative energy left by bad news, arguments, or visitors with less-than-positive vibes. This works for any kind of housecleaning that involves physical cleaning, from mopping your kitchen floors to scrubbing the toilet.

For a minor boost, just set your intention before you get going, and then clean as you normally would. Or if you *really* want to integrate magick into your housecleaning, try adding in another tool from your magickal toolbox—throw in a few herbs as well.

As we all know, different herbs and plants have different magickal uses. What you might not have realized is that many of the plants that are used magickally for cleansing have those properties in the mundane world as well. For instance, most citrus—like lemon and orange—have antibacterial qualities, in addition to their pleasant aroma. And magickally, both lemon and orange are useful for clearing away negativity.

So I like to take a few drops of lemon essential oil and add them to my cleaning water. This way, I get a two-for-one punch from my cleaning. There are lots of other magickal oils that can be used this way as well. A good book to use if you want to learn more about magickal housecleaning is *The Magical Household: Empower Your Home with Love, Protection, Health and Happiness* by Scott Cunningham and David Harrington.

Step Four: Create Magick with Food and Drink

While you've got your magickal herbs out, we might as well step into the kitchen. We all have to eat, right? And much of the time that means preparing food and drink for ourselves, and sometimes for our loved ones. There are a number of easy ways to integrate magick into this everyday task, without doing anything more complicated than you would normally do, or putting forth much in the way of extra effort.

As with housecleaning, much of the power of our kitchen alchemy comes from our adding focus and intention to the mundane actions of cooking and food prep. If you're like me, and try to eat healthy, you can focus on your intention to support your body with the foods you prepare.

But you can also take it a step further, and add an element of alchemy to your kitchen magick, by mixing in herbs and other elements, and focusing on their magickal properties as you do so.

Here's an example: most mornings, I drink hot mocha (chocolate with a little organic coffee mixed in) for breakfast. You would think

that the only magick involved is the caffeine helping me to transition from sleepy to awake—but you'd be wrong. When I put the ingredients into my electric cocoa maker, I add in a little cayenne pepper and a bit of cinnamon. The pepper is for energy and creativity (and maybe a little passion) and the cinnamon is for prosperity. As I mix all the elements together, I say aloud my intention to bring these things into my day. And voilà—instant kitchen alchemy.

You can create the same magickal effect by adding herbs to any dish, or even picking ingredients that have the power you are looking for. Many everyday foods also have magickal properties. A couple of good books for research are Gerina Dunwich's *The Wicca Garden: A Modern Witch's Book of Magickal and Enchanted Herbs and Plants* and another book by Scott Cunningham, *Cunningham's Encyclopedia of Wicca in the Kitchen*.

And while you're at it, don't forget to be grateful for the food that blesses your table. You might want to take a moment before you eat to give thanks for the animals and plants that give up their essence to sustain your body, and the people who labor to bring it to you.

Step Five: Replace Negativity with Positive Thoughts and Actions

Most witches are familiar with the basics of the Law of Returns, which states that what we put out into the world is what we get back. But we often forget to pay attention to our smallest thoughts and actions, and they get lost in the hustle and bustle of our everyday lives. How often do we carelessly say something mean to someone else, or even to ourselves? (For example: "I can't believe you did something so stupid!" Or "I'm an idiot!")

Most of these thoughtless words or gestures are pretty insignificant when taken by themselves. But when you add them up at the end of the day, or the month, or the year, they can start to amass a hefty weight of negativity. And if the Law of Returns is true (and I think it is), that means we've brought a lot of not-so-good stuff back into our lives as well.

So here's an experiment for you to try as you set out on the path to becoming an everyday witch: for one day, just one, really pay attention to all your thoughts and all your words (at least as much as you can manage without driving yourself into a wall or getting yelled at by your boss). I think you might be shocked by how many times something negative slips in when you least expect it.

Then, try replacing each one of those negatives with a positive. For instance, if you catch yourself thinking "I hate my coworker," immediately replace the thought with "he's just a flawed human being, no one is perfect," or something to that effect.

If you do this often enough, you will find it becomes a habit, and eventually you may not need to do it at all. Just think of what you could accomplish with all the positive energy you are gifted with instead.

Step Six: Make Little Things Count

A while back, I wrote a book called *The Goddess Is in the Details: Wisdom for the Everyday Witch*. Much of the book was devoted to ways we could integrate our spiritual beliefs with our everyday lives; to walk our talk, as it were.

I believe it is important, as witches, that we live our lives as the best possible human beings we can be. After all, we are all a part of the divine and so a little bit of deity should shine out of each of us through our actions and our treatment of others.

This doesn't mean we have to be perfect or completely unselfish all the time—we *are* human, after all. But it does mean that we should go out of our way to help others when we can and practice random acts of kindness on a daily basis if the opportunity should arise.

My wish for you is that you will be your best self every day, and strive to learn and grow as you walk the particular road that is your path to being an Everyday Witch. Blessed be.

Deborah Blake's *bio appears on page 88.*

Illustrator: Paul Hoffman

Witchcraft Essentials

PRACTICES, RITUALS & SPELLS

Make a Witch's Kit of Your Own

Susan Pesznecker

The good witch is always prepared—ready to work magick, enchant the moment, or craft the perfect charm. One of the best ways to ensure this kind of readiness is to assemble a kit—a sort of toolbox that is kept close at hand, stuffed with supplies and ready to use on the go.

The word "kit" comes from the Middle English: from Middle Dutch *kitte*, which is a wooden vessel of unknown origin. This was later applied to other containers, particularly a soldier's equipment. Many professionals today talk of being "kitted out"—ready with the right clothing, materials, and equipment.

As you prepare to build your kit, begin by considering when and how you might use it. Ask yourself the following questions:

- What tradition do you follow, and what sorts of basic supplies might you carry as a result? A nine-foot cord? A copy of the Pledge of the Goddess? A set of stones?

- What kinds of magick do you work with? Do you do a lot of ritual? Spend time journaling? Watch the movement of the stars? Work with tools of divination? Craft magickal tools? Work in nature? Your kit should reflect those basic predilections.

- Do you want to keep all or most of your basic paraphernalia together in the kit so that it becomes a master storage space, or do you prefer to craft a smaller version—a "portable" collection that you can take when you leave your usual workspace?

- If you're creating a portable kit, what's the purpose? Do you want to be ready to gather natural specimens while traveling? Prepared to create a spontaneous ritual or a runecasting?

Your answers to these questions will help you start thinking about the kind of kit you'll create. Grab a paper and pencil and jot down your thoughts. Start a list if you have ideas about what you'll put into the kit. I'm going to make some specific suggestions, and you can come back and forth to the list as needed.

The Kit Itself

Your kit can be simple or richly adorned, practical or arcane, large or small, or just about anything in between. The kind of physical container you choose will depend on its contents and how and when you'll use them.

If you'd like a full-service kit that holds all of your basic tools and materials and provides both storage and some portability, I suggest a soft-bodied toolbox, like construction workers or carpenters might use. I use a big soft-sided tool case from Duluth Trading (see Resources); it's made of tough materials and is filled with around

ninety different loops, pockets, and zippered containers, as well as "fold flat" sections to provide a work surface. I adore it, but I am admittedly one of those people who likes to have everything organized and in its proper place. Look for a cushioned laptop space, if a computer is an important part of your daily workings.

If you'd like something a little smaller and a little less organized, consider a backpack, briefcase, or messenger bag. Most of these have only a few pockets or compartments, but you can increase the efficiency by separating your contents in different-sized containers and pouches.

Smaller still? Many camera cases are good, too, especially those with moveable dividers. Outdoor supply stores sell zippered kits of ripstop nylon; these contain netted sections, loops, small containers, and zippered compartments, and are great for organizing smaller collections of items (see REI in Resources). Art supply stores sell fabric holders for drawing, painting, and sculpting materials. These roll up and tie shut. A good friend of mine uses a small velvet drawstring bag to hold a miniaturized set of supplies. The bag lives in her car and travels everywhere with her. She calls it her "Port-o-Pagan."

Is appearance especially important to you? Check second-hand or vintage clothing stores for old ornate purses, satchels, briefcases, or traveling jewelry holders. Many magick shops have special "witchy bags" designed especially to carry materials. Or you might peruse the pattern catalogs in fabric stores and look for bags that you can make yourself out of whatever materials you choose.

Perhaps you're theme oriented. You can have fun with this. The healing-oriented witch might choose an old doctor's bag, or craft a traditional "medicine bag" out of a large piece of leather or animal skin, gathered at the corners and tied shut to enclose all items. A kitchen witch could select and decorate a picnic hamper, while a ritualist might choose a decorated or painted wooden trunk, and an herbalist might select a deep-sided basket with a drawstring liner. Don't forget to consider colors, too.

An interesting option, for those who will use their kit mostly for ritual or altar work, is to employ a small hard-sided briefcase or lunchbox. When opened, the inside of the case serves as a portable altar or workspace. Art or deity images can be glued to the inside of the upper lid as a backdrop and a pentacle or altar surface painted or glued onto the interior bottom surface. Store materials within, and voilà! It's a portable altar that is ready to use.

Whatever type of kit you choose, make sure there's a way to keep it closed, and even locked, especially if it includes anything that is private or oathbound. Double-zippered toolbags and backpacks allow use of a small luggage-style lock (find these in outdoor and travel stores, such as REI). Tying a knotted cord around the kit will hold it shut and will slow down anyone who is unauthorized to open it. Tie with a square knot; this four-cornered knot provides balance and elemental protection and also takes a bit of time to undo.

Inside the Kit

The following is a list of materials and supplies for a basic magickal kit, one that most magickal folks will find useful as a starting point. Be sure to choose sturdy, unbreakable items.

- Small notebook
- Written copy of any important prayers, blessings, invocations and so forth that are not committed to memory
- Pens, pencils, and colored pencils
- Candles
- "Strike anywhere" matches
- Charcoal tablets
- Thurible (a small iron cauldron, abalone shell, or a flat stone)
- Loose or stick incense, or a smudge stick
- Tokens or statues to represent your elements, watchtowers, patrons, and so forth
- Mat or small tablecloth, for creating a clean surface anywhere; ideally this should be large enough to sit or even lie on
- One or more divining tools (runes, Ogham sticks, a small tarot deck, a mirror)
- One or more magickal stones or crystals (quartz, turquoise, and obsidian are a good starter trio)
- One or more vials of essential oil (lavender and rosemary are solid multipurpose choices)
- Container of sea salt
- Small cup or chalice

- Small plate

- Sticks of white chalk

- Cornmeal or tobacco, for Earth offerings

- String or cording

- Scissors

- Small tape measure

- Spoon

- Magickal tools as desired (e.g., wand, athame)

- Small first-aid kit

With the materials in the above kit, one could "outline" a circle or ritual space, create spontaneous ritual, write and work a spell or charm, bless or empower a tool, make an offering, cleanse or consecrate an area, carry out a divination, meditate in comfort, or complete just about any magickal purpose. The contents will need to be adjusted according to your own preferences and purposes. For instance, you need to decide which stones, herbs, or oils to include, but this is an excellent basic list to begin with.

Cleanse the materials using the method of your choice. For a four-element cleansing, pass them through the heat and smoke of a candle or some burning herbs (air and fire elements) and then anoint or sprinkle with a bit of salt water (earth and water elements). Consecrate the kit to your purpose by speaking words of beseechment and telling it of the adventures you'll have together. Then, expose it to the light of the Full Moon. Renew the cleansing and blessings as needed.

Make It Your Own!

While I provided a good master list, you'll want to make your own additions, tailored to your own practices. Here are a few suggestions:

The garden witch is happiest among her plants and works all or much of her magick there. She might add a trowel, a pair of garden shears, garden gloves, a packet of compost or granular plant food for offerings, a small piece of garden statuary (e.g., the Green Man, Demeter), and a small bowl for offerings to the wee folk.

The naturalist witch adores nature and spends long, happy hours padding through the countryside in search of nature-based sightings and materials. This kit might include field guides, containers for collecting items (small boxes, plastic bags, etc.), a pocketknife, magnifying lens, compass, rock hammer, and camera.

The kitchen witch works magick in the home and kitchen. The home-based kit might include measuring spoons, a selection of spices (pepper, cinnamon, and others), a stash of herbal teas (especially chamomile and mint), bath tea bags, a sharp knife, rock salt, and a mortar and pestle.

The divining witch is always watching for signs and auguries. Additions to this kit are focused on diving tools: multiple sets of tarot cards and interpretive booklets, Ogham sticks or runes with a fabric mat for castings, a small scrying mirror or crystal ball, and stones or shells for tossing may be added to this kit.

The healer witch is prepared to tend his fellow humans. His kit might require a thermometer, a set of chakra stones, vials of color-charged waters, a set of essential oils, and healing stones (amethyst, bloodstone, and fluorite are good examples).

The herbal witch is ready to stir up a potion or poultice, as needed. Measuring spoons, mortar and pestle, empty tea bags, gelatin capsules, a carrier oil (sunflower is excellent), essential oils, grated beeswax, cheesecloth, and spoons for stirring may be added to this kit. If much work will be done in the field, you might add a one-burner backpacking stove and a small saucepan.

Have some fun personalizing your kit and making it your own by using fabric paints or permanent markers to add symbols or even words in an arcane alphabet. Attach beads, patches, fringe, or whatever else suits your fancy and makes your kit a unique work of art. I like to add some token to my kit for each adventure or outing we've completed together.

A Small All-Purpose Kit for Everyone

Are you looking for a small, all-purpose kit that will leave you ready to deal with virtually any magickal necessity, while taking up minimal space? The following kit represents "magickal minimalism" at its finest, but it will help you be prepared for just about any magickal eventuality.

In a small pouch or reticule, assemble the following, using small containers or zippered plastic bags for each:

1. **Salt:** Preferably coarse sea salt; this can be used for cleansing, blessing, consecration, protection, or as a representation of the earth element.

2. **Obsidian, tiger-eye, or turquoise:** one piece, for overall protection. Obsidian is also useful for both grounding and banishing.

3. **A twelve-foot piece of cord:** tie a loop in one end and then tie knots in the cord at 12-inch intervals. To inscribe a nine-foot

circle, pound a small stick into the ground, slip the loop over it, and stretch the rope out to reach nine feet (nine knots). Use this to form a circle; with a stick at its center, it is a giant math-style compass.

4. **A smudge stick**: use sage, cedar, or juniper, or a bundle of loose dried herbal material are good options and useful for smudging, blessing, purification, warding, and invoking elements of air and spirit. They can also be brewed into an infusion or strewn to honor or give offering to a natural space.

5. **A small candle**: use blue for healing, harmony, and peace; green for vitality, prosperity, and the natural word; yellow for energy and enthusiasm; red for passion, courage, and physical power; white as a safe generic color. Also carry strike-anywhere matches. The candle can be used to light the smudge, provide a working light, invoke the fire element, and serve as a scrying focus. It also can be an important part of a ritual. For safety, include a glass votive with the candle.

6. **A small container of water**: use spring water if possible, that has been charged in sunlight or moonlight. Use to invoke the water element, to create anointing or cleansing mixtures, or to brew infusions for drinking.

7. **A small vial of lavender essential oil**: used externally in a rub or infusion, this is an all-purpose remedy that soothes jangled nerves, decreases inflammation of all kinds, speeds relaxation, and promotes sound sleep and sweet dreams. Magickally, lavender essential oil fosters peacefulness, diminishes stress, and counters against dark or chaotic magick. (Rosemary oil is a good optional oil; it has stimulating and invigorating effects and promotes mental clarity and memory.)

8. **Paper and pencil**: use to write spells or charms and to keep the always-important records of magickal and herbal workings. The

paper can also be folded into images for altar use, while the pencil can be charged and enlivened as a wand, for directing energy.

9. **A 12-inch square of aluminum foil:** fold several times to create a thick square. This yields a safe surface for burning herbs; it also can be bent into a bowl shape or unfolded to cover a larger altar space.

10. **A clear quartz crystal:** ideal for channeling energy and for healing and purification.

These items provide the ultimate in being prepared, but don't hesitate to mix and match, adding other materials that may be particularly important to you.

Naming and Consecrating Your Kit

While the label of "kit" is simple and sustaining, you may be looking for something more. Try using the words valise, satchel, pouch, reticule, or *portmanteau*. Even better: give your kit its own name, followed by a naming ceremony in which you state its name, list its assigned tasks and responsibilities, and charge it to its new role as your assistant. Add a secret symbol or token in honor of the kit's new status. Consecrate and energize, using your favorite process (I use full moonlight).

Have fun building your kit and watching it grow to become one of your most vital magickal tools!

Resources

Duluth Trading. http://www.duluthtrading.com. A wonderful source for soft-sided toolbags and for all sorts of woodcrafting tools.

REI. http://www.rei.com. A source for outdoor gear of all kinds, zippered nylon bags, small containers, and travel locks.

Susan "Moonwriter" Pesznecker's *bio appears on page 88.*

Illustrator: Bri Hermanson

Green Witch Initiation

Susun S. Weed

"I am a witch; I am a witch; I am a witch." I repeated this mantra as Zsuzsanna Budapest wound a red cord three times around my waist and tied it. It was my first initiation as a witch, and I was thrilled. With the two other women who were initiated that night, I formed the Coven of the Warm November.

After meeting for two Full Moons and reading *The Feminist Book of Lights and Shadows*, the Coven of the Warm November decided to initiate ourselves on the holy day of initiation: Candlemas, February 2. In the Catskill Mountains, where we live, February is the middle

of the winter. Nonetheless, we stripped off our clothes, cast our circle, and danced—clad in sky and goose bumps. Then, we broke the
ice on the stream and, each in turn, squatted down in the frigid water and declared ourselves witches. Initiation completed, we hastily
opened our circle and dashed inside to shiver by a warm fire.

Two years later, our coven expanded to include four other feminist witches. New Moon Coven (our new name) met at the dark of
the Moon, when the Sun and the Moon are in the same astrological
sign. We practiced candle magic, experimenting with color, noting
the differences between sizes and number of candles. The smaller
the candle, the faster the results of our spells, we found. A spell on
a tiny birthday candle, asking for a mean boss to chill out, brought
news that the man in question had just had a massive heart attack!

We practiced magic together for a year, learning to sense elemental energies, raising cones of power, and becoming adept at building altars in the woods, before we decided we needed an initiation. Older and wiser, we envisioned a warm ritual, though still in winter's heart. Each in turn, we relaxed in a bathtub of steaming water festooned with rose petals and lavender blossoms. As the spirit moved us, we stood up, stepped out, and announced our Craft name.

At least, that was the plan. But I didn't have a magical name. I lay back in the flowery, steamy water. "What is my name?" I whispered to myself. "What is my name?" I silently pleaded with my guides. "What is my name?" I yearned to know. But nothing came to me. I couldn't move. I couldn't get up. My coven sisters' patience began to wear; they were envisioning the cakes and cider waiting for us in the kitchen. My skin was puckering, but I wasn't ready to stand up and step out. I didn't have a name. I pulled more of my body under the water. I squeezed my eyes shut.

Gentle but firm hands drew me up. I stepped over the edge of the tub, terror in my heart. As my foot touched the bath mat, my mouth, seemingly of its own volition, announced: "I am Iona." "Oh no," I cried inside. "What have I said? I own a car? I own a house? I own a what?" It was more than a decade later that I found the isle of Iona, the magical fairy isle, and realized that the fairies had named me.

Our coven unraveled after two more years. I practiced as a solitary. It suited me. I relished the freedom. I felt my magic grow strong. My trance work deepened.

Life is not all magic, though. My own teaching, plus planning workshops at the Wise Woman Center, took much of my time. I invited Zsuzsanna Budapest to teach as often as she wished. This allowed me to absorb her Dianic teachings and make them mine. With her guidance, I brought the Goddess to the foreground of my life. My altars became lavish affairs. My rituals expanded gloriously.

I became more public about being a witch. I crafted rituals for others, though I still practiced as a solitary.

One year, out of the blue, without preparation, Zsuzsanna turned to me in the middle of her workshop and announced: "I will initiate you as a high priestess this evening." I was stunned. I was delighted. Lady Iona became one of her thirteen high priestesses.

Zsuzsanna charged me with two tasks during the initiation: I was to initiate any women who desired it as a Dianic witch, no restrictions; and I was to initiate at least one woman as a high priestess within the next two years—but not just any woman. There were restrictions.

I hung out my shingle, which said, "I initiate green witches." Over the decades hundreds of women have found their way to the Wise Woman Center to be initiated as green witches. My initiation ritual bears little resemblance to the early initiations I experienced. There is no tying of red strings, no breaking of ice, no hot baths in herbs. Just simple, powerful, natural, goddess-lovin' magic.

I Invite You to Come with Us for the Initiation

First, eat breakfast; then take the time to adorn yourself with flowers and finery. Zsuzsanna reminded me often: "It's a nighttime religion." But nighttime rituals require a fire, a problem on my land, so I do my high magic initiations at noon.

Now, find your place in the processional line: oldest first, following in age order. We chant "We Are Sisters on A Journey" as our procession winds through the woods.

We are sisters on a journey, singing now as one,
remembering the ancient ways, the women and the wisdom,
the women and the wisdom.

We turn left at the Hecate Way and begin our climb, pausing at the trance gate, where I bless each woman.

We are sisters on a journey, singing in the sun;
singing through the darkest night, the healing has begun,
begun, the healing has begun.

The land I live on is rough and rocky, interspersed with swampy areas, buttressed by cliffs, and shining with water seeping from hundreds of springs. There is only one flat place: a cliff top where the bedrock is richly covered with startlingly green mosses and bonsai-beautiful trees. This is the Mesa. It is the physical and spiritual center of my land, my ritual space, my heart. Quarried stone is piled up like a psychedelic playhouse for a giant. Glacial scratches imprint our bare feet. An altar of rocks is graced by a bow, painted stones, bones, and flowers in season. Diana/Artemis lives here. A wind chime sings from the ancient oak that arcs over one side. Moss carpets reach to the very edges of the rocky cliffs, which drop down dozens of feet to ferny corners.

Hum with us as we take the last few steps to the top of the Mesa and stand before the trance gate. A short birthing ceremony created by Zsuzsanna carries us into sacred space. Move through the encircling arms and listen to our chant:

From a woman you were born into this world;
from women you are now born into this circle.

I am the last woman to come through the circles of arms. Allow me to lead you in a dance widdershins, chanting Marie Summerwood's "Let It In, Let It Go." Unwind the energy. Three times round the altar, chanting and dancing, we go. Then we reverse the order and dance around to the right. The casting of our magical circle has begun.

Take your place at one of the four directions; each element is called by those whose Sun sign places them in that quarter.

Powers of the East, Powers of the Air, Be here now!

We call the elemental energies: air, fire, water, earth. The youngest woman invokes Above. The oldest woman invokes the Below. I invite you to call in your personal guardians, guides, and beloved ones; then to go deep within, to sense your vibrating, vibral core.

... a woman came to the Wise Woman Center asking permission to look for an owl feather in my forest. There are owls aplenty here, but finding a feather is not so easy ... She slept that night on the mesa, and asked for a dream that would help her to use the feather she had been gifted with.

From that core I ask you to spin a thread, a tendril, a fiber, and to send that connector to our center, where we will weave our threads, gather our tendrils, braid our fibers together and spin ourselves into a spiraling core of power. We become aware that we are one. One with each other. One with the Earth. One with all that is. Our heartbeat becomes one.

From this shared center, I summon the magic. It rises above us; it roots beneath us. A double cone of energy surrounds us. The circle is cast. We are now beyond time and space. I warn us all that it is unwise to be outside of time and place in any state other than perfect love and perfect trust. Take a step forward and say:

I *enter here in perfect love.*

Then to take another step forward, and say:

I *enter here in perfect trust.*

We have arrived at the juicy middle. If you wish to offer a song, a dance, a poem, or a portrayal of your goddess archetype, now's the time to do so. Or you may wish to add a twig to "the Nest," a place for incubating dreams, brooding on plans, and envisioning the forms to come. You may also wish to place a leaf or a bit of bark in the "Well," a circle of rocks where problems are transformed into allies.

Decades ago, a woman came to the Wise Woman Center asking permission to look for an owl feather in my forest. There are owls aplenty here, but finding a feather is not so easy. Five hours did bring success. She slept that night on the Mesa, and asked for a dream that would help her to use the feather she had been gifted with. It was Summer Solstice eve. The rising Sun woke her, and she was moved to lay a row of rocks pointing to it. To complete her gratitude give-away, she returned that December and spent the night on the Mesa again. On the morning of Winter Solstice, she laid another line of rocks pointing at the rising Sun. The ends of the lines met just at the edge of our ritual space. This angle graphically shows the movement of the Sun (where I live) between the longest day and the longest night. It is our "Angle of Becoming."

I take my staff and step into the Angle of Becoming. I raise a silk scarf in front of my face. Hand-painted, this scarf was a gift from the Sisterhood of Shields. It came to me from Amylee and carries an especially potent personal magic. Behind its shield, I step further in the glamour of high priestess; I become Lady Iona. As I lower it, slowly revealing my face, I feel myself transformed.

Raising the scarf shield again, I await you, the first initiate. I am guided by the fundamental meaning of initiate. To initiate is to begin. This initiation is not a reward, nor does it signal any particular knowledge, skill, work, or worth. When I initiate a green witch, I see myself as the opening of a door, the revealing of a path, the sounding of the opening notes of a lifelong symphony. To accept initiation is to agree to begin or continue to walk the way of the witch. And I define witch thusly: a witch is a woman whose religion is her life and whose life is her art. A green witch's art is the wise use of the green.

You step into the Angle of Becoming and stand before me. I slowly lower the scarf, allowing my inner vision to show me your aura, your chakras, your essence, your truth, your body. As the scarf reaches the ground, I bow before your feet. You are the Goddess; I am your high priestess. Standing, I look into your eyes.

"What is your name?" I ask. The question is expected. You know that I will ask you three questions. Perhaps you have a magical name; perhaps you prefer the name your mama gave you.

"Are you here of your own free will?" I continue. "Has anyone led you to believe in any way that being initiated is required of you, or that you must do this?" I question further. "Has anyone threatened you in any way, overt or subtle, to be initiated?"

It is vital to me that each woman I initiate is there entirely of her own choice, with no fear and no expectations. Your affirmative answers reassure me. I gently turn you away from me and toward the women in the circle.

"May I embrace you in the name of the Triple Goddess?" I ask, as I place the silk scarf around your shoulders. Then I say:

She has a thousand names and a thousand faces. Maiden She is.
Mother She is. Crone She is. In every place, in every time,
She shows Herself to us in every woman. If we wish to see the Goddess
right now, we need only look upon this face. If we wish to call the Goddess
right now, we need only say _____

(I repeat the name you have chosen.)

Dearest Goddess, I am Your High Priestess, I stand in support of You.

(I hold you lightly; I gently squeeze your upper arms.)

Feel my support _____,

(I repeat the name you have chosen.)

And tell us your commitment.

I have previously asked each woman to envision a commitment and to bind it in time. I have reminded each woman that keeping a commitment, no matter how small, builds personal power; and that breaking a commitment, no matter how large, erodes power. This is one of the most important things that the Craft teaches. In society at large, commitments are treated casually, broken at a whim. Or commitments are made that are too far-reaching to ever be achieved.

I repeat your commitment; then I ask if I have heard you clearly, correctly, and fully. If you say yes, then your sisters say together:

I hear your commitment _____ (and repeat your name).

I then turn you toward me. I kneel before you and paint the big toenail of your left foot with sparkly green polish, and say:

From this day forward, each step you take, you take on the path of the green witch. Each word you speak, you speak as a green witch. Your thoughts and plans, your hopes and dreams, are now the thoughts, plans, hopes, and dreams of a green witch _____ (I repeat your name).

I rise, kiss you on both cheeks, and remind you:

As you will, with harm to none, so mote it be. Blessed be.

You step out of the Angle of Becoming. The next women rises and steps in. As I begin the next initiation, you may go to the grove

of Lady Beauty, to be instructed in glamour, or return directly to your place in the circle.

Initiations complete, I step out of the Angle of Becoming. We release below, above, north, west, south, east, and finally, the center, and I say:

The Circle is open, but unbroken. May the love of the Goddess be ever in your heart. Merry meet and merry part, and merry meet again.

We dance and sing, laugh and hug, then meander back to the house for lunch.

. . . .

I'm so glad you could join us. Can you stay for the lesson on spell crafting? Here is one of my favorite spells that is safe enough for beginners, but plenty potent even for those witches who have much experience.

Green blessings until we meet again, in person, in our dreams, or in print.

Spell to Attract Good Fortune

This spell is especially useful when dealing with legal matters.

"I _____ (insert your full name) exist in the universe.

"_____ (insert the full name of one person you are struggling with) exists in the universe."

Repeat this statement in full with the name of each person involved. Include your lawyer, their lawyer, the judge or magistrate, even the jurors if you know their names. Then, say:

"There is a connection between us that brings about the greatest possible good."

I generally combine this with candle magic, lighting a candle of appropriate size and color as I engage this spell. Repetition is a key element. I do this spell every night until the matter is resolved.

Susun S. Weed's *first book,* The Wise Woman Herbal, *was published in 1985. Since then, her work has appeared in peer-reviewed journals and magazines. Her worldwide teaching schedule includes herbal medicine, the psychology of healing, nutrition, and women's health. Learn more about Susun at www.susunweed.com.*

Illustrator: Tim Foley

Brigid's Cross

Linda Raedisch

Brigid. Bride. Brigantia. Brigandu. She may be as old and as universal as fire worship itself, but because she was also the goddess of smithcraft, this article will not attempt to place her any earlier than the Iron Age. Though Brigid, as we will call her for now, is associated almost exclusively with Ireland, her traces are clear to see throughout the British Isles and on the continent.

In Germany, this feisty little fire goddess, or at least one of her devotees, was preserved in the German epic *Das Nibelungenlied*. Both the *Nibelungenlied* and the Norse *Volsunga Saga* were written down somewhere around the beginning of the thirteenth century. Both treat the same subject matter, but because the *Volsunga Saga* preserves a little more of the ancient traditions, it is there we will search for our virgin flame-keeper.

Brynhild

The *Volsunga* poet calls her Brynhild—*bryn* means "mail coat" in Old Icelandic. Rather than rehash the soap-operatic plot of the *Volsunga Saga*, let us examine Brynhild's ongoing relationship with fire. Her association with smithcraft is clear enough; she is dressed in a helmet and skin-tight coat of mail when the dragon-slayer Sigurd first stumbles upon her, drawn to her mountaintop bower by a blazing light. Brynhild, we learn, is a fallen valkyrie, or "chooser of the slain." She has been stabbed not to death, but to sleep, by the god Odin after she chose the wrong king to be slain. Odin has induced this enchanted sleep by means of a magic thorn, just like the witch who caused Sleeping Beauty to prick her finger on a spindle and later be surrounded by a hedge of thorns.

> **Brynhild's ring of fire and the fairy-tale princess' forest of thorns place them in the same ancient tradition as the Irish Brigid, the foundations of whose firehouse still stand in the green grass of Kildare.**

But it is not the slumber itself that is Brynhild's punishment; it is the loss of her virgin, valkyrie status, for Odin has sentenced her to marriage. In an effort to commute her sentence, Brynhild vowed she would marry no man who knew fear. (You see, she had not yet met Sigurd!) In the story of Sleeping

Beauty, the waking of the princess is the end of the story; for Brynhild, it is just the beginning.

At first, the hero and the valkyrie are quite smitten with each other. He frees her from enchantment, she teaches him runes. Before parting atop Hindarfell, they promise to marry. But, as in all soap operas, stuff happens. Sometime later, we find Brynhild seated in a hall surrounded by a steadily burning hedge of fire, awaiting the man who knows no fear. We all know that's Sigurd, but the hero has forgotten his promise. Sigurd crosses the flames unscathed, as only he could do, and claims the bride on behalf of his friend Gunnar.

Brynhild's ring of fire and the fairy-tale princess' forest of thorns place them in the same ancient tradition as the Irish Brigid, the foundations of whose firehouse still stand in the green grass of Kildare. The twelfth-century historian Gerald of Wales relates that this house, in which nineteen nuns plus St. Brigid tended a fire of hawthorn wood, was surrounded by a man-eating hedge. One unfortunate male who managed to cross it went mad and died shortly after. Another got a foot over the stockade before his more level-headed companions pulled him back. That man lived, but the offending foot was instantly withered.

As for poor Brynhild, she must now marry Gunnar, and she is not happy about it. She rages and sulks through the rest of the saga, finally conniving to bring about the death of her beloved but forgetful Sigurd. Her third and final communion with fire occurs on the dragon-slayer's funeral pyre into which she throws herself in a voluntary act of suttee. (Though she had married Gunnar, she remained Sigurd's spiritual wife.)

What are we to make of the uncompromising Brynhild? As a valkyrie, she seems to have belonged to a cult that demanded, if not virginity, then at least chastity. (In Chapter 29 of *Volsunga Saga*, Brynhild drops off her "daughter by Sigurd, Aslaug," at her foster father's house, so she and Sigurd must have done more than talk atop Hindarfell.) Brynhild's valkyrie education invested her with specialized knowledge—herbs, runes, poetry—and probably special status. Behavior like Brynhild's was certainly not the norm for a woman in early German society. That their home was the barren mountaintop, their realm the sacred, makes it clear that personalities like Brynhild's lived outside the social sphere.

One thing we know for certain about Brynhild, or Brunhilda, is that she was not the invention of either the *Nibelungenlied* or the *Volsunga* poet. The first written reference to the sleeping valkyrie comes from the hand of Bishop Bardo of Mainz, or his secretary, in 1043, about two hundred years before either poet put pen to parchment. Bardo's document describes a nearby rock formation that was known to the locals as "Brunhilda's Bed."

Gerald of Wales tells us that the fire had been burning there by the sacred oak in which Brigid made her first nun's cell since the time of the Virgin.

This Brunhildisfelsen, as it is known today, is not unique. Once upon a time, there were Brunhilda's stones, chairs, and beds scattered throughout the German countryside, always in high places. At the turn of the last century, a few still served as hearth places for the peasants' Shrove Tuesday bonfires. How exciting it would be to know exactly what went on in prehistory in those barren mountain fastnesses, what songs were sung, what knowledge was passed on. Did a sisterhood of valkyries tend a sacred flame as did their cousins the Vestal Virgins in ancient Rome? For clues, we must look beyond the continent to Ireland.

For there, the old fire goddess survives not in a poem but in the person of St. Brigid. Many scholars agree that it is impossible to define where the saint begins and the elder goddess leaves off, but the Christian Brigid is so much milder and more generous than the unswerving, petulant Brynhild that it is tempting to believe the goddess, too, was somewhat kinder than her continental incarnations. Perhaps the milder climate of Ireland had a mitigating effect on her temperament. Then again, she may have merged with one of the goddesses already in residence there. Ireland's many energetic stone monuments, sometimes called bridestones, testify to the fact that there was already a lot of religion going on in Ireland before the bearers of Celtic language and culture landed on Irish shores.

Many if not all of the stories, miracles, and wonders set down by St. Brigid's seventh-century biographer, Cogitosus, relate directly to pre-Christian practice. Brigid came into the world on February 1 with

flames shooting out of her head. Just as Sigurd thought he saw a fire burning on Brynhild's mountaintop, the locals, looking up from their Imbolc festivities, mistook the saint's birth for a house fire. But most notable to us is the perpetual flame which burned at her monastery at Kildare. In her lifetime, Brigid herself was one of the tenders of this flame, taking her own shift every twentieth night. On the other nineteen, the fire was tended by one of her nineteen nuns. After the saint's death, the nuns noticed that on the twentieth day the fire required no tending; Brigid continued to pull her shift.

Gerald of Wales tells us that the fire had been burning there by the sacred oak in which Brigid made her first nun's cell since the time of the Virgin. Since Christianity did not arrive in Ireland until several centuries into the common era, this would point to a Pagan Irish fire cult. Even if we are to take old Gerald's account with a grain of salt, the appearance in the story of oak and hawthorn, two trees near and dear to the Pagan heart, suggests that Kildare had long been the site of some sort of ritual activity.

It is interesting to note that, unlike many early saints, Brigid was not a martyr. There simply was no opportunity for martyrdom in Ireland, and the erstwhile Pagans segued into their new religion with little fuss. On the continent, the great oak Irminsul was chopped down to prevent its worship by the Germans. In Kildare (*Cill-dara*, meaning "cell of the oak"), the sacred tree was simply turned into a church. In much the same way, Brigid the saint took over the mantle of Brigid the goddess—a mantle which, it is said, the saint could hang on a sunbeam.

Brigid's fire flickered on through the Viking raids, only to be put out by Henry VIII. It was re-lit in 1993 and continues to burn under the watchful eyes of the Brigidine Sisters in Kildare. Though they have rekindled the flame, the sisters have thankfully not resurrected the deadly hedge around it.

If you've opened this book, you've probably already chosen a path—now stick to it! If you feel yourself straying, use the flame to invoke a little of your inner Brynhild to get yourself back on track.

Brynhild's was an unswerving code, akin to that of those most famous flame-keepers of all, the Vestal Virgins of ancient Rome. Here, purity was paramount. The Vestal who was careless enough to lose her virginity was buried alive. (Nor did the goddess Vesta ever give her virgins a day off!) The stockade around Brigid's firehouse, as Gerald describes it, seems to be a vestige of the continental fire goddess' ferocity, but on the whole, Brigid's cult was a forgiving one. There is no record of any of her nuns being cast out, let alone buried alive. In fact, one of Brigid's miracles, according to Cogitosus, involves a strayed and consequently pregnant nun. Brigid intervenes, causing the unborn child simply to evaporate from the womb so the nun need not leave her order. No pain, no shame.

What meaning should a perpetual flame hold for us today? Should we approach it like Brigid, or like Brynhild? In some ways, we have fewer worries than our ancestors. We know the days will start to lengthen in February and that they will do so regardless of our actions. We no longer have a physical need for a perpetual flame. No bow-drills or tinder boxes for us; we can start a fire whenever we want to by turning a dial or striking a match. But the ease with which we control fire does not prevent us being drawn to it, as the dragon-slayer was drawn to Hindarfell.

A candle flame is as effective a point of focus today as it was in those early days. Nowadays, however, it is no longer necessary to abstain from sex in order to tend your personal flame. Instead, we can adopt a symbolic and far more meaningful purity. We can be true to ourselves and to our purposes. Light a candle and swear an oath to yourself to pursue your Campbellian bliss. If you've opened this book, you've probably already chosen a path—now stick to it! If you feel yourself straying, use the flame to invoke a little of your inner Brynhild to get yourself back on track. But remember, as Brigid did, that straying is inevitable.

Triskelion
Tea-light Holder

Brigid's firehouse was not the only place to host her sacred flame. The windowless houses of old Ireland boasted hanging lamps adorned with both solar and vulvar symbols, suspended by three chains from the rafters. And when the hearth fire was banked for the night, the embers were divided into three parts, at the center of which Brigid was believed to dwell. Though lamp and hearth place have disappeared, most Irish homes still keep a straw Brigid's Cross in the kitchen or above a door or window.

The most common form of Brigid's Cross is the one with four arms which St. Brigid was supposed to have woven on the spot out of rushes in order to convert a dying Pagan. But you will also see a three-armed version, which some believe is the older of the two. Traditionally, the four-armed cross was kept underneath the thatch of the house while the triskelion was placed in the byre for the protection of the livestock.

The following craft is inspired in part by Brigid's straw triskelion and in part by the more serpentine forms seen on the Newgrange kerbstone and other prehistoric monuments in Ireland.

You will need aluminum foil, scissors, tea light, and a pencil or chop stick (optional).

Rip off a length of aluminum foil about eighteen-inches long. You can use any kind of foil, but the heavier it is, the less likely it is to tear when you don't want it to. Fold the foil lengthwise into thirds. (If you want to make the four-armed cross, fold it into quarters.) Cut along the fold lines to make three narrow strips. Fold each strip into thirds again lengthwise, shiny side out. Now gently twist each one along its length as if you are making a breadstick.

Pick up one of your "breadsticks," grasp the end and start curling it over itself as if you are quilling or making a cinnamon bun. If you want, curl it around a pencil or chopstick, but not too tight. Leave about the last five inches straight. Do the same with the other three pieces.

Arrange the four "fiddleheads" you have made into a triangle (or a square if you are making the four-armed cross). The center triangle should be large enough to place a tea-light inside. Hook the straight ends around one another to hold everything in place. It's important to make sure that the "cinnamon buns" on the outside are all curling in the same direction. If you find you've made yours withershins rather than deosil, don't panic: just turn it over!

Now place your candle in the center and enjoy the play of light over the scintillant surface.

References

Bitel, Lisa M. "St. Brigid of Ireland: From Virgin Saint to Fertility Goddess." Presented at Fordham University, 2001, http://monasticmatrix .usc.edu/commentaria/article.php?textId=6.

Byock, Jesse L. *The Saga of the Volsungs.* New York: Penguin Books, 1990. (Translation, introduction, notes.)

Cahill, Thomas. *How the Irish Saved Civilization.* New York: Anchor Books, 1995.

Dames, Michael. *Mythic Ireland.* New York: Thames and Hudson, 1992.

Fischer-Fabian, S. *Die Ersten Deutschen: Ueber das Raetselhafte Volk der Germanen.* Germany: Bastei Luebbe Taschenbuch, 2003.

Herrmann, Paul. *Deutsche Mythologie* (Fifth Edition). Germany: Aufbau
   Taschenbuch Verlag, 2001.

Ord Brighideach International: www.ordbrighideach.org.

"St. Brigid's Cross": www.crosscrucifix.com/brigid2.htm.

Tate, Karen. *Sacred Places of Goddess: 108 Destinations.* San Francisco: Consor-
   tium of Collective Consciousness, 2006.

Linda Raedisch *lives with her two daughters in a house made of books.*
She teaches paper crafts and writes about religion, holidays, and the arts.

Illustrator: Kathleen Edwards

Coven of the Dead

Melanie Marquis

A lone, I light the candles. Alone, I cast the circle. Alone, I kneel down in the dirt and call on the Moon to join me. By all appearances, I'm a solitary practitioner, but looks can be deceiving. My inner circle in fact consists of several dear friends, disembodied but with spirits raging with magick and passion nonetheless. They're dead, but they are not gone.

Many solitary practitioners wish, at times, that they could have a little help with their magick, a few companions to lend their energies and to share those mystical experiences. It is sometimes hard for witches to find coven mates in their own community, but there's a world of friendly spirits waiting beyond the veil of death who are more than willing to lend a hand.

Together, my coven mates and I work spells, craft magickal tools, share in worship, conduct rituals, and divine hidden truths. They take me into the realm of death, and I share with them my living body. Such rituals are enjoyable for the dead as well as the living; they create a space of communion and empowerment where the division between life and death blends into unified spirit and magickal power. Working magick with the dead broadens awareness. It's a mutually beneficial relationship, a the catalyst to evolution. Dead or alive, we can always make progress.

Of course, it's not like I posted a flyer and set up my coven of the dead overnight. It took years of believing in disembodied spirits before I ever had the notion to work magick with them. In fact, it wasn't my idea at all. The first time I found myself working magick with the dead was several years ago when I was outside on my patio casting a much-needed spell for protection. As I sprinkled black pepper around my candles, I caught a whiff of a scent quite different from the strong spice I had in my hand. It was the unmistakable fragrance of a recently deceased friend's favorite cologne. I turned around and felt his presence glide out from behind a nearby tree. I spoke his name, and as if in confirmation, his spirit moved to stand beside me, and I knew I was meant to return to the magickal work at hand. As I raised up a protective energy to shield my loved ones, a cold sensation entered my body and coursed through me, an intense surge of power poured into me from the disembodied soul at my side. I took in the energy and wove it into my spell, shaping it into an unbreakable barrier to bind my foes. When we were done, I thanked my friend, we said goodbye, and the spirit lifted. Had I any reservations about believing, I would have halted the spell and run away in fear or denial, and the experience would have been impossible.

I grew up in a haunted house, and early encounters with the spirit world allowed me to reach adulthood with little doubt that the dead may choose to linger among us, and those spirits who do move on can still make house calls now and then. When I was seven years old, I lived in an old two-story wooden white house that had once been used as a trackside hospital for railroad employees. There were remnants of the track running through the backyard, and I loved digging around in the dirt in search of old, rusty railroad ties. Though I didn't realize it at the time, those relics provided me with my first experiences of psychometry. Whenever I happened upon one of the large metal spikes and held it in my little hands, I would get a vision of our house in the days that it was a hospital. I'd see a nurse running frantically up the stairs. I'd see a man, gray and grizzled, lying on a narrow bed and moaning, his leg bandaged and his suffering eyes streaming.

And then there was the balcony. The first time I stepped out on it, I said to my sister, "There's a man out here." I felt the fear and regret emanating so strongly from his presence that going out on the balcony scared me, but I felt guilty leaving the dead man out there all alone. So I would get my courage up and visit him from time to time. I would stand beside him on the balcony and look down until fright overtook me and sent me scurrying back to my bedroom. The day we moved from that house, I went out on the balcony one last

time. I remember waiting until no one was around so I could speak out loud. "I'm sorry you fell," I said to the spirit. "But you scare me and I can't stay here. You can go now, but you can't come with us."

To me, the existence of disembodied spirits was an undeniable fact. They shared my house, noticed me on my walks through the cemetery, and made their presence known in the tumbleweeds rolling through the Arizona desert surrounding my childhood home.

My mom introduced me to automatic writing and showed me how to use a talking board when I was about ten, paving the way to deeper mediumistic interactions. Over the years, I learned to use other spirit communication tools and developed my own methods, using tarot cards, candle flames, and dream work to exchange information with the dead.

I enjoyed these conversations, but I wanted more. I realized that if disembodied spirits can talk with us, they'd probably like to do other things with us, too.

I fell in love with painting as a teenager. By the time I was in my mid-twenties, I was showing my artwork in venues across town. I had a bad habit of lining up art shows before actually making the artwork, and I never would have been able to complete my paintings in time for these frequent showings without the assistance of several dead artists. I'd simply get out my paints, offer myself up as a vehicle, and let the spirits have at it. I had a hunch that since painting with the dead was a spiritually enriching experience, there were probably other beneficial ways to interact with those on the other side. I wasn't sure how that would work exactly, but I believed it was possible, and that belief is what made it possible.

The encounter with my friend's spirit out on my patio, that very first time I worked magick with the dead, opened my eyes to new options. I began experimenting to find new ways to bring the dead into my magick circle. I researched, practiced, and followed my intuition until I developed a variety of techniques and traditions for going beyond spirit communication into a richer shared experience.

Today, I work different types of magick with different groups of spirits. There are four doctors I call on for help with healing magick. They're easy to summon. I cast the Circle, and then I make contact with my spirit guide, mentally joining him among the craggy standing stones surrounding our special meeting place. I ask him to invite the doctors to come to my ritual. Soon, I feel their presences join me, three older men from eras past and one younger man seemingly from more modern times. I thank them for their attendance, and thank the God and Goddess for allowing the interaction. I light a candle or lay out a photo or other token to represent the person in need of healing. I ask the God and Goddess to keep strong the spark of life within the sick, to remove any barriers impeding recovery. Then I ask the disembodied doctors for their aid. I tell them the name of the person in need of help, what they look like, and where they live. I ask the doctors to go to the location and do what they can to heal the illness. My consciousness travels there as well, and I glide my hand over the person's body, mentally drawing out and banishing pain, disease, and infection. I sense the doctors are ready to get to work, so I leave them to it, my thoughts coming back to the Circle. Folk magick keeps me busy while I wait for their return. I sprinkle herbs, manipulate poppets, burn anointed candles, or use other techniques suggested by the supplies I have on hand. Whatever form the spellwork takes, I don't drive the magickal energy to its apex until I feel the doctors are finished with their healing session and are once again with me. "Would you like to help with this part, too?" I ask, and then I resume the spell. I thank the doctors and my spirit guide for their help, I thank the God and Goddess, and I dismiss the Circle.

Another group of spirits helps me cast protective charms. Two young friends who passed too soon, and a dead relative from the Wild West, attend these rituals. I summon each of these spirits in different ways, and it can take several minutes to get the attention of each one. One of the young friends, the first disembodied soul I ever practiced magick with, in fact, usually comes directly when I mentally "call" him and seek him out. When he's hard to reach, I play some of his favorite music and I try again until he notices me. The other young man I reach by spilling red wine on the earth and scratching his name along with a cat symbol in the wet dirt. The old relative I call by reading out loud segments of the cowboy poetry he wrote during life. Once we're all assembled, I mentally convey a description of the dangerous situation and the need for protection. I ask the two younger fellows to protect the people in danger, and I ask the old cowboy to stop the person who's causing the danger. I cast my own shield of protection around the victim and I cast binding spells to hold back the perpetrator. I ask the spirits to help me in this, and I ask the deities to support our efforts.

Of course, some magickal activities I prefer to do with less familiar spirits. Dancing with the dead is one experience that's best shared among strangers. Sometimes I put on dark music, like Bauhaus, and sometimes I play music I think will appeal to the particular type of spirit I'm hoping to welcome. I paint my body with skulls, Odin's rune, spirals, or other glyphs associated with the Underworld. I start

the music, turn out the lights, and invite the spirit or spirits to come into me, moving my body however they like. My ego gets pushed behind the veil and the essence of the departed slips into the spotlight. I feel like an observer watching a dream unfold, aware but not entirely present. With energy raised to its height, we switch back to our own sides of existence and direct the power we each conjured back into the whole of reality, working magick both above and below to achieve global aims, lend strength to the forests, power to the animals, and endurance to the people.

I also occasionally like to work magick with spirits who happen to be hanging around the graveyard. I sprinkle water on a handful of graves that I find intriguing, and then in a circle on the ground surrounding me. I set out sage, wormwood, mushrooms, or other "death herbs" to attract the attention of the spirits. Then, I lay out whatever other magickal supplies I have with me, and I invite any friendly spirits present to use me as a medium for their magick. Many of the spirits I meet in graveyards are intent on bringing comfort to their living loved ones. I let the spirits guide my movements and lead the ritual, instructing me in the sprinkling of herbs and the manipulation of tools. As I work such spells, I often feel a loving, comforting energy flowing out of me, directed toward unknown persons whom I picture quite clearly. I feel my energy and that of the deceased wrapping around the surviving friends and relatives, invoking a perma-hug effect that allows sadness to lift. I ask the deities to guard and distribute the spell, delivering fresh bursts of the comforting energy to the living loved ones whenever it's especially needed.

Through these many varied experiences, my disembodied coven mates have taught me that the dead can invoke some forms of magick that the living cannot, just as the living can weave spells in ways the dead cannot. The difference between awareness and sensation is the difference between death and life. The dead can heal, protect, convey information, send symbolic messages, send comfort, and a host of other things, but they cannot feel, they cannot taste, and they cannot smell. The living body is a precious vehicle that allows us to perceive and experience individual parts of the universe in a variety of ways. In death, we are more aware of the rules and operations of this universe, but we are no longer a part of it, as we are no longer apart from the united essence of it. Free of the body, we are boundless, but without bounds, there is no container in which to hold the life force, no machine for the batteries to operate. Magick with the living offers the dead a vehicle through which to act, and magick with the dead provides the living with the ultimate insider assistance.

Melanie Marquis *is a full-time witch and writer. She's the founder of United Witches global coven, and she also organizes a Pagan group in Denver, Colorado. She's written for many New Age and Pagan publications, including* Pentacle Magazine, Circle Magazine, *the* Wiccan Pagan Times, *and the American Tarot Association's quarterly journal. A non-denominational witch, she specializes in practical spellwork, tarot, and spirit communication, teaching a personalized approach to the magickal arts. Visit Melanie's Web site at www.unitedwitches.org.*

Illustrator: Rik Olson

The Magical Benefits of a Vegetarian Lifestyle

Tess Whitehurst

The reasons to make the switch to vegetarianism go far beyond altruism. The vegetarian lifestyle is delicious, fun, and great for your health. And since you're of the Pagan persuasion, I've got even more reasons for you: eating a vegetarian or vegan diet can clarify and hone your intuition, connect you deeply with yourself and the oneness of all life, *and* amplify your magical power. Here's another biggie: it's quite possibly the single most significant step you can take toward minimizing your ecological footprint. See what I mean? Not yet? Let me explain . . .

Supercharged Health

First things first: according to the well-known and well-respected Oxford Vegetarian study, vegetarians live longer and healthier lives than meat-eaters. To be more precise, mortality rates for vegetarians in the study were found to be lower in these three categories: cancer, heart disease, and all causes of death combined. While I don't mean to imply that cutting out meat automatically means you're a healthy eater, these findings are significant, and similar findings have been consistently produced by numerous other studies.

But being healthy isn't just about living longer. It's about feeling vivacious, joyful, and beautiful. And, as witches, we're all aware of how much more magical power and spiritual aliveness we possess when we feel active, attractive, and vibrant.

The Intuitive Edge

For the last six years, I've eaten a largely vegan diet. During that time, my intuition has been activated and awakened to the point where I'm now doing intuitive readings for others professionally. I definitely give some of the credit to my vegan diet for these developments, and I've heard similar sentiments from a number of other professional psychics and intuitive counselors.

How does eating a vegetarian or vegan diet enhance your intuition? Mainly, it's vibrational. Many factory-raised animals live in horrific conditions and are killed in inhumane ways. This, of course, means that their flesh is filled with negative vibrations, including fear, sadness, and depression, all of which create darkness and energetic congestion in our heart, third eye, and crown chakras (all chakras which must be open for clear psychic perception). Not only that, but when we energetically sensitive people ingest flesh-foods, we often unconsciously choose to shut down our psychic abilities in order to shield ourselves, at least on the conscious level, from these negative vibrations.

Most of us are not in a situation that *demands* that we kill an animal, eat its flesh, or wear its skin or fur.

It's also physical: digesting meat takes up a lot of life-force energy because the human digestive system evolved over the millennia to handle light diets made up of largely plant-based foods. This energy drain and "brick in the belly" feeling can cause us to feel cloudy and heavy, which naturally diminishes our intuitive abilities.

Spiritual Stimulation

We are all one. Each of us is one with the whole, with all of life. Many Native American tribes have traditionally honored this wisdom, so when their situation demands that they kill an animal, they are careful to use every part of every animal they kill. A number of tribes also perform ceremonies honoring the spirits of the animals they eat, and some of their myths are centered on respecting the equality of these animals.

Most of us are not in a situation that *demands* that we kill an animal, eat its flesh, or wear its skin or fur. When we consciously decide *not* to do these things, we are, like the Native Americans, making the choice to honor and connect with the wisdom that we are all one. While some of us might also hunt in a very conscious manner, or raise farm animals with great care, both of which are also honoring this wisdom, most of us can have our nutritional and clothing needs met by non-animal-derived products. Also, as many Native Americans had to learn, it's emotionally challenging to hunt or slaughter an animal while simultaneously treating it with respect and love.

Additionally, fresh, raw fruits, vegetables, and herbs (especially organic ones) are virtually overflowing with powerful spiritual energy. If you're anything like me, making them into your main food staple will strengthen your aura and amplify your inspiration, joy, energy level, magical power, and conscious connection to the Divine.

Honoring the Earth

Here's are some facts: animal agriculture contributes to the destruction of rainforests, the drying up of grasslands, the compromising of underwater ecosystems, and the erosion of topsoil. Switching to vegetarianism is a more powerful way to help the planet than switching to a Prius (and it's cheaper)! We have the power to not

only reduce global warming and pollution, but also to *reduce world hunger*. And it's as simple as making the switch to a plant-based diet. Talk about a powerful way to honor our Mother!

Some Guidelines for Making the Switch

If you're ready to make the switch, there are a few things you might like to know. Below, you'll find a little practical guidance and I'll address some common concerns about getting started.

Eat your greens. You must eat fresh green veggies! Most new vegetarians think protein is the only thing to worry about, but iron and calcium are important, too. I get sluggish if I don't eat enough fresh greens—especially leafy ones. If you want a concentrated shot of minerals, try a juice drink made with green veggies such as spinach, wheatgrass, parsley, and cucumber. And did I mention that your skin is going to glow?

Get a new perspective on protein. When you make the switch, it seems like everyone asks you: "Are you getting enough protein?" As it turns out, it's very difficult to *not* get enough protein—especially if you cut out refined white sugar and white flour (non-nutritional filler foods) and focus on eating any or all of the following:

- Raw fruits and vegetables (especially avocados, artichokes, and leafy greens)

- Nuts, seeds, beans, and sprouts

- Grains like oats, rice, and quinoa (also sprouted grains)

- Soy products (though many people are sensitive to these)

And here's bit of advice that a veteran "veggie" gave me when I was a rookie: When nonvegetarians ask you if you're getting enough protein, just smile and ask them if *they're* getting enough *vegetables*. Most likely, the answer will be no, whether they admit it or not.

Don't obsess. When you're overly concerned with not letting a morsel of animal-based food through your lips, you're not starting out on the right foot. With this mindset, a single splurge can make you feel like you've failed and cause you to give up altogether. If, on the other hand, you take it one meal at a time, eating as few animal products as possible during each, you're setting yourself up for success. You might also want to ease your way into the vegetarian lifestyle, cutting out one thing at a time. For example, you might start by cutting out red meat; then, after a week or a month, eliminate white meat,

and finally, seafood. Later, if you feel inspired, you might choose to cut out eggs, and then dairy. Still, if you find yourself eating a piece of salmon or a slice of cheddar at a family barbecue, don't freak out. Just fully enjoy each bite, and, at the next meal, continue doing your best to eat a mostly vegan or vegetarian diet.

Do a supermarket stakeout. If you're worried that you'll miss certain foods, you might want to make a list. Write down everything you're concerned about giving up. Then take a leisurely trip to the supermarket (preferably one with a good health food section) and investigate what might fill those same cravings. You might purchase these as an experiment to see if they will, in fact, work for that purpose. My hunch is that you'll discover that vegetarianism opens you up to a whole new world of culinary delights. For example, there are some really delicious vegetarian hamburger patties on the market, as well as vegetarian versions of most other types of meat. There are also tons of milk alternatives to choose from, including soymilk, rice milk, oat milk, hemp milk, and almond milk. Oh, and if you like to cook, scout out some recipes online and maybe look through a vegetarian cookbook or two!

Be prepared for negative reactions. I've found that many people perceive the choice to eat a vegetarian diet as a direct threat or insult to them. The reason for this, I think, is that eating habits are deeply ingrained and touch on people's

... **simply saying "I don't eat meat" can sound like an insult to someone's whole way of living. I am here to tell you this: don't take the bait! As intimidating as it can seem when someone reacts in a negative way to your personal choice, remember that you once ate meat yourself.**

self-image as well as their feelings about their family and culture. In other words, simply saying "I don't eat meat" can sound like an insult to someone's whole way of living. I am here to tell you this: don't take the bait! As intimidating as it can seem when someone reacts in a negative way to your personal choice, remember that you once ate meat yourself, and everyone evolves in his or her own time. As much as you can, have compassion for people and don't let them convince you that you meant to be insulting in any way. You were merely stating a fact. Of course, if they have questions, you can answer them. But remember that as soon as you say an angry word, you're perpetuating the belief that vegetarians are self-righteous and judgmental. Also, if you're concerned with making a point, coming from a place of compassion and patience is the only way to go. That being said, don't worry if you have trouble with this one at first. It can be tricky to keep your cool, especially if you come from a family of meat-eaters. (I should know.)

Spread the love. The more people who go veggie, the more harmony there is on the planet! And the best way to spread the vegetarian love is to be a walking advertisement. Infuse your life with magic, living your dreams and being your healthiest, happiest, and most authentic self.

Resources

Appleby, Paul N. et al. "The Oxford Vegetarian Study: an Overview." *The American Journal of Clinical Nutrition,* www.ajcn.org/cgi/reprint/70/3/525S.pdf.

Cousens, Gabriel. *Conscious Eating.* Berkeley: North Atlantic Books, 2000.

Flinn, Angel. "The Vegan Solution: An Ideal Whose Time Has Come." *Care2.com,* www.care2.com/causes/environment/blog/the-vegan-solution-an-ideal-whose-time-has-come.

Freston, Kathy. "Vegetarian is the New Prius." *HuffingtonPost.com,* www.huffingtonpost.com/kathy-freston/vegetarian-is-the-new-pri_b_39014.html.

Nerburn, Kent. *The Wisdom of the Native Americans.* Novato, CA: New World Library, 199.

Virtue, Doreen, with Becky Prelitz. *Eating in the Light.* Carlsbad, CA: Hay House, 2001.

Tess Whitehurst *is an advocate of self-love, self-expression, and personal freedom. Her first book,* Magical Housekeeping *(Llewellyn, 2010), is now in stores. She is also columnist for* New Witch *magazine, an intuitive counselor, and a feng shui practitioner. Her Web site, www.tesswhitehurst .com, and free monthly e-newsletter,* Good Energy, *include simple rituals, meditations, and musings for everyday magical living. Tess lives in Venice Beach with two magic cats, one musical boyfriend, and a constant stream of visiting hummingbirds.*

Illustrator: Neil Brigham

Magical Transformations

Everything Old Is New Again

Self-Discovery in Fairy Tales

Elizabeth Hazel

Once upon a time . . .

This is the opening line for fairy tales, which follow a fairly strict formula. The details may change, but the pieces and parts follow a certain order. This is because, for a long time before anyone wrote them down, fairy tales were transmitted orally, a process that culminated in the Grimm Brothers' collection of fairy tales.

The standard fairy tale format makes it easier to remember and tell. For the purposes of this writing challenge, it's good to distinguish between formulaic fairy tales and myths, which are not.

Several years ago, I wrote a personal fairy tale as a self-discovery exercise. I am going to share the process with you. As pieces of the fairy tale format are described here, your job is to plug personal imagery into the formula's blank spaces. Spontaneous creative choices open a portal to hidden emotions, and can also shake unexpected solutions out of your brain. This is particularly true when you're in a rut, stuck, or frustrated with your situation. This journaling-type method fares best when approached in an imaginative, non-judgmental way, and when formula choices are spontaneous and even humorous. So get pen and paper or PC, loosen up your brain, and prepare to write.

The Main Character and Plot Line

The first step is to identify the main character of the tale, which is you. Your fairy tale name should be based on solid tradition. If you're a woman, pick a name that involves a color description (Rose Red can be Magenta Plum or Sparkling Chablis), a distinctive item of clothing (Red Riding Hood can be Baggy Jeans), a job title, or a distinctive feature that ends with suffixes like "locks" or "ella." Male fairy tale monikers can be indicative of brain power or birth order, like Simple Hans, Clever Bob, or Young Bill. Sometimes physical characteristics or personality traits are included in men's names, like Husky John or Timid Tim. These names may be the opposite of the true trait: Simple Simon may prove to be quite smart in the story.

The second step requires the most ingenuity. You must transform your troubling personal situation into a fair tale–styled metaphor. The manner in which a problem is personified serves as the basis for conflict, testing, and personal struggle for the main character. A flaw or challenge has to be built into the situation.

The situation at the heart of your fairy tale should be very obvious. Something must be lacking (money, a job) or desired (a partner, travel, knowledge), or there must be a condition that needs resolution (a sick child, a relationship problem).

For instance, if you're struggling with family issues, turn your family members into a clan of troublesome dwarves. The dwarves pester the main character, or trap him with a horrible job obligation. If you're struggling with a relationship, turn the partner into someone who is locked away or hidden and has to be found through magical means. A difficult job situation with a troublesome boss could be transformed into a story about a cobbler who has trouble making shoes for the king. Or if you're looking for a perfect career, create a character who has to find some tool or treasure to rescue a kingdom.

The main character's situation has to be untenable, which means the character cannot continue along on the same course. The situation that you decide upon will propel the main character (the fantasy-you) into action.

The first paragraph is an introduction to the main character and identifies the challenge or flawed situation the character contends with.

Once upon a time, a girl named Scribblielocks and her three cats, Wheezer, Teezer, and Meeser, lived in a house made of feta cheese. While quite delicious, every day a bit of the house crumbled. The cats were tired of eating cheese, and poor Scribblielocks was exhausted from fixing the leaks in the roof all by herself. She was so busy filling the cracks in the walls with humus and putting fresh cheese on the roof that she didn't have any time to write her columns or books, or go out and meet nice new people, or even have a date once in a while. All of her clothing smelled like cheese, so when she did get out of the house, dogs followed her around everywhere.

Scribblielocks is an appropriate fairy tale name for a frustrated writer, and at the time, my house required multiple expensive repairs, including a new roof. Creating a house of feta cheese was my metaphor for a building that seemed to be crumbling. But since the feta cheese house is described as delicious, Scribblielocks doesn't want to leave her house; she just wants it fixed so she can have a life.

So One Day . . .

Now the main character takes some action. There are three main formula choices:

1. Go into a forest (a metaphor for entering into the heart of a mysterious issue).

2. Go to a nearby castle (seeking an opportunity or challenge).

3. Go to market (seeking an exchange or transaction).

The main character could also leave to venture on a journey with a vague destination, an option that would appeal to people who really don't know their destination and need to discover one! Or there could be an unexpected knock on the door, so the action comes to the character.

The main character must encounter someone else almost immediately. This needs to be a fateful character:

- A fairy godmother

- A troll under a bridge

- A group of dancing fairies

- Ladies who turn into swans

- A king with a son or daughter who needs rescuing

- Elves making cookies

- An old man, a witch or wizard (good, bad or strange, depending on the plot line)

- A talking animal, ghost, or angel

This fateful character can be helpful, threatening, or confusing; and the interaction must propel the main character into further choices or actions. Don't be afraid to make this character a bit silly; be playful! The fateful character may threaten or take something away from the main character. The fateful character may also give the main character a magic tool, directions or instructions, or a challenge.

It is at this point of a fairy tale formula when Jack swaps his cow for magic beans and Cinderella gets a dress for the ball. Sometimes the main character selflessly helps out the fateful character and gets rewarded later in the story. He or she may perform thankless tasks that others have refused.

If you're including a magical device (whether animal, mineral, or vegetable), it can be empowering and help the main character fulfill his objective, but how it works may not be clear at this point. Fateful characters don't always give good instructions, and they *never* explain why they're there. This adds an element of the unknown that forces the main character to act on trust or faith.

So one day Scribblielocks was walking in the forest, when who should appear but her fairy godmother. And what a fairy godmother she was! She was dressed in a white Roberto Cavalli two-piece suit, her platinum locks were teased into a huge beehive hair-do, and she was driving a Jaguar V12 convertible.

"Oh, dah-link," she said to Scribblielocks, "a nice girl like you shouldn't look so sad. Here, lemme give you these three things: a bag of magical seeds, a vial of this special perfume, and this sealed envelope." She handed Scribblielocks a pouch containing all of these goodies.

"Gee, overdressed fairy godmother, that's real sweet of you," said Scribblielocks, "but what's it for? Don't you have a magic wand for fixing stuff?"

"Don't be snarky, Scribblie. The Fairy Godmothers Association strictly limits wand use for fashion emergencies," her fairy godmother explained, "and while you're a mess, you got bigger problems. Your house is turning into a cheese ball."

"So whaddo I do with all this stuff?" Scribblielocks asked in exasperation.

"Take the seeds and sprinkle them on your roof. Trust me, you won't worry about leaks anymore."

"Oh, great," said Scribblielocks. "How 'bout the perfume?"

"This stuff is incredible. It leaves Love Potion #9 in the dust," the fairy godmother said, while waving wildly with her perfectly manicured hands that were encrusted with gaudy cocktails rings from QVC. "Put on a drop of this perfume, and guys will fall all over you, and agents will hunt you down begging to represent you."

"Wow. Can I get more?"

"You haven't even used this bottle yet."

"Good point. So what's the envelope for?"

"Hide it in your house somewhere and forget about it."

"What does it do?"

*"You'll see." And with that, the fairy godmother put the pedal to the
metal and blasted off in her Jag.*

As you can see, my fairy godmother is a cross between Fran
Drescher and Joan Rivers, and the dialog sounds like an old com-
edy routine. Maybe I was channeling George Burns that day. Scribblielocks has to take the effectiveness of the magic tools on faith,
and the fairy godmother offers no explanation for her timely intervention, or why she's driving a Jaguar through the forest.

STORMING THE CASTLE

At this point, the main character has to proceed as instructed, moving on to the next step of the challenge. Decide on the time span
you'd for like your character to work through this process—days,
weeks, or years. Or a vague time span can be suggested (for example,
"Some time later").

The main character may meet other characters or encounter
characters, animals, or obstacles predicted by the fateful character.
Perhaps you'll have monsters to trick or vanquish, a glass mountain
to climb, or caves to explore. This is the middle of the story, and the
main character is in the thick of the challenge, or must put magical
tools or devices to use.

Scribblielocks went home and followed her fairy godmother's instructions. Within a few months, royalty bird nests covered her roof
like a blanket, and the birds started laying golden eggs. The leaks
stopped, and golden eggs started piling up. Scribblielocks and the
cats did a happy dance as she bagged up the eggs and took them to
the local gold exchange.

*Then Scribblielocks started wearing the magical perfume oil, and got
asked out on a bunch of dates. One night when she was walking home,*

a wild-eyed woman leapt out of a dark alley, and begged to be her literary agent. The potion was so strong that the agent insisted that she receive only five percent of Scribblie's royalties. Scribblielocks signed on the dotted line. Soon her books were on the New York Times best-sellers list.

Life at Scribblielock's house got better every day. She met a great guy, JonPaul, who had always wanted to live in a house made of feta cheese and bird's nests, and got along with Wheezer, Teezer, and Meeser because he bribed them with fried chicken livers and vanilla ice cream.

As you can see, once she put them to use, the tools she got from her fairy godmother were quite effective. Scribblielock's basic problems (a crumbling home, a shortage of money, need for a literary agent, and a nonexistent love life) were fixed when she used her magic tools. A new character, a boyfriend, entered the situation. All of this in three short paragraphs! Scribblielock's tools worked quickly and effectively.

Living Happily Ever After

Finish the story with the main character meeting the challenge:

- The magical tools do their job
- The destination is reached or quest fulfilled
- The monster is overthrown
- Evil is averted
- The person is rescued

Your main character deserves a happy ending, so provide one. But a few choices and options still remain at the end:

- The main character may need to have a second encounter with the fateful person, and may get some explanation or resolution.

- The main character may return to his or her original location, or may upgrade and move into the castle.

- The main character may go on his or her merry way, or enjoy benefits from overcoming a challenge, like having access to a treasure, getting married, or having a happy family and domestic harmony.

It is at this point that some mysterious element can be resolved, especially if you weren't quite sure of the purpose of some magical tool given by the fateful character. Resolve this in a fun, creative way, perhaps by inventing a benefit that the main character doesn't expect.

Eventually, Scribblielocks asked JonPaul to move in with her. So JonPaul (who was very hunky) brought his stuff to her house. As he was putting his CDs by her stereo, he came across an envelope that was addressed "To the Guy who Shacks Up with Scribblielocks." Puzzled but curious, JonPaul opened it and looked to see what was inside of it. A short note was enclosed, and on it he read:

"This is a note from Scribblielock's fairy godmother to the guy who shacks up with her. Treat her like a princess for the rest of her life or I will turn you into something horrible. Use the enclosed gift – you won't be sorry and you'll make Scribblielocks very happy."

He looked in the envelope and found a gift certificate for a twelve week ballroom-dancing class for two. JonPaul took Scribblielocks to the dance classes and they had a blast. JonPaul never mentioned the envelope he'd found, but it didn't matter.

While the Sun was shining, Scribblielocks wrote feature columns and books, and JonPaul kept the feta cheese house in good shape, fed the

royalty birds, and carried the gold eggs to the gold exchange. Scrib-
blielocks loved watching his bulging muscles when he did this job.
Every evening they did the rumba in the moonlight, and the three cats
purred until they were all asleep. And they lived happily ever after.

Although the fairy godmother gave three items, I didn't know what the letter was for until I wrote the final paragraph. This was a wild element in the story, one that wasn't under the control of either Scribblielocks or the fairy godmother. It took a new character to make the magic happen.

Tips for the Writer

Keep descriptions short and the action moving. Nobody cares how many leaves are on a tree unless the hero or heroine has to count them as part of a challenge. The most important thing is to finish the story! Getting mired in excessive details can prevent that goal. Write a quick outline of the story to keep yourself on track.

Fateful characters provide a timely nudge for the main character. Magic tools can be anything, and don't have to make sense. A mysterious tool that appears early in your tale leaves something begging for a creative solution at the end of the story, and this may be the most enjoyable part of your writing experience.

Try creating a composite character by blending characteristics of different celebrities or literary characters. Keep dialogs short and pithy, as lengthy discussions slow down the story and tend to offer too much information.

Write the story straight through, without looking back. Let your creativity take over, and go with the flow. Analyzing, while you're in the midst of your process, can snuff out your creative flow. You can go back when you're finished and tweak problem spots.

Later On...

Put your story aside after writing it, perhaps in an envelope you can find later. Your fairy tale marks a specific moment of your life; it describes your state of mind, personal conditions, hopes and fears. The fateful character is a vessel for things lurking in your subconscious mind; possibly traits you want but feel you don't have. This character may also display hidden aspects of your personality that you aren't acknowledging yet.

Put the main character on a straight line going from the challenge to fulfilling the terms of his quest. Feel free to make your metaphors outrageous or zany, and leave room for miracles and magic to fill in the details.

Even though it may not seem terribly profound when you write it, the metaphors you choose for your story can yield fruitful insights in retrospect. And the best part of all is that personal fairy tales may come true! Plant this creative seed, and like Jack's magic beans, it may grow.

Elizabeth Hazel *is an astrologer, tarotist, artist, and mystic scholar. She is the author of* Tarot Decoded *and* The Whispering Tarot, *and writes horoscopes, feature columns, and articles. Liz is the editor of the ATA Quarterly Journal and has lectured in the United States and Britain. She has also officiated at open community sabbats in the Toledo area. Visit her Web site at www.kozmic-kitchen.com.*

Illustrator: Tim Foley

Kheperu: Ancient Egyptian Practice for Modern Covens

M. Isidora Forrest

Cool moonlight streams into the circle, falls upon the altar, glitters on the silver jewelry upon the breast of the high priestess. Her eyes are closed. Her arms and legs are flung wide—as if she would abandon her body by sheer human desire. She breathes softly and deeply. Before her, the high priest kneels:

> "I invoke thee and call thee, mighty Mother of us all. By seed and root, by bud and stem, by leaf and flower and fruit, by life and love do I invoke thee to descend upon this thy servant and priestess!"

The witches begin a low humming as the high priest continues to invoke the moon goddess by her many names, asking her, praying her to descend—now!—into the body of her priestess.

Then a sharp intake of breath. The high priestess's breathing has become ragged. Moonlight catches in her hair and illuminates her body. Her hair stands on end. Her dark eyes snap open, staring strangely. The atmosphere within the circle is changed. Every one of us feels it. Excitement in the pit of the stomach. Anticipation. Truth.

The high priestess looks into our eyes, into our hearts, and begins to speak the Charge of the Goddess:

Whenever you have need of anything, once in the month, and better it be when the Moon is full, then shall you assemble in some secret place to adore the spirit of Me, who am queen of all the witches . . .

We have "drawn down the moon." The woman who was our high priestess is—for this brief and sacred moment—the Goddess incarnate, and she gives us her blessings.

Drawing Down the Moon

The practice usually known as "drawing down the moon" is a traditional part of many modern Wiccan and witchcraft esbat and sabbat celebrations. Depending upon the particular tradition, it may be part of every ritual gathering. Janet and Stewart Farrar, influential authors of A *Witches' Bible Complete*, included it in the general opening ritual that precedes every ritual. In *The Spiral Dance*, the equally influential Starhawk said of this invocation:

> To invoke the Goddess is to awaken the Goddess within, to become, for a time, that aspect we invoke. An invocation channels power through a visualized image of Divinity. In some covens, one priestess is chosen to represent the manifest Goddess to the rest. In our covens, she is invoked into each member of the circle.

The concept of "drawing down the moon" is not a modern one. Our knowledge of the term comes from the Greco-Roman period, when the witch-women of Thessaly, Greece, were famous for it. Thessaly is on the Greek mainland, north of Delphi and south of Olympus. Drawing down the moon was a common-enough practice that philosophers and satirists could refer to it in their works without specific definition. Plato mentions it, as do the Latin writers Lucan and Horace, sometimes simply referring to "those Thessalian women who draw down the moon." Clearly, the technique was well known and evocative even in the highest intellectual circles.

Unfortunately, we don't know exactly what the Thessalian witches themselves believed about the technique; none of them wrote about it. But from the few references to the practice from other writers that remain to us, it seems to have been a way to intensify magical practice; to add effectiveness to the ritual.

Greco-Egyptian Magic

Whether the Thessalian witches meant what modern Wiccans do by the term, we do not know. However, there *is* a direct ancient correlate to the modern practice of drawing down the moon, or as it is known in modern ceremonial magic traditions, the Assumption of God and Goddess forms. It is to be found in ancient Egypt. And a simple connection between Egyptian magic and Greek magic is quite easy to make. Egypt was *the* great civilization of the ancient world, and Egyptian priests were renowned, not only as great magicians, but also as being exceptionally wise keepers of mysteries. Scholars agree that Egypt's defining influence on the way magic, both spiritual and practical, was worked is evident in Greek texts and extends deeply into Greek culture. Researcher Garth Fowden, author of *The Egyptian Hermes, A Historical Approach to the Late Pagan Mind*, states plainly that most Greek magic cannot be explained except by Egyptian antecedents.

THE EGYPTIAN TECHNIQUE

The ancient Egyptians did not leave us a name for this technique. I have called it *Kheperu* (see my book *Isis Magic*), which is Egyptian for "transformations" or "forms." The root of the word means "to be, to exist, to form, to create, to bring into being, to take the form of someone or something, and to transform oneself." If it was not what the Egyptians called the technique, Kheperu is certainly an appropriate name. For convenience, that's what I'll call it in this article.

We find the technique throughout Egyptian religious literature and in practical magical texts that record for us the intersection of Egyptian and Greek magic. Here is one of my favorite examples. It is Formula 485 in the Coffin Texts:

I am in the retinue of Hathor, the most august of the Gods, and She gives me power over my foes who are in the Island of Fire. I have put on the cloak of the Great Lady, and I am the Great Lady. I am not inert, I am not destroyed, and nothing evil will come to pass against me. I am the Great One Who Came Forth From Re, I was conceived and borne by Shesmetet, and I have come that I may weave the dress for my mistress. The dress is woven by Horus and Thoth and by Osiris and Atum; and indeed I am Horus and Thoth, I am Osiris and Atum.

The deceased puts on the cloak of Hathor and *becomes* Hathor. He is both the weaver and the wearer of this magical covering of the Goddess. He calls it her cloak and her dress; modern witches and magicians might call it the Goddess's astral form.

IDENTIFYING KHEPERU

It's relatively easy to tell when we are witnessing the technique of Kheperu. Most simply, whenever we find the deceased, the priest/ess, or the magician claiming *to be* a particular goddess or god and speaks in the first person, we are likely to be witnessing Kheperu. It is the voluntary taking on of the astral or imaginal form of a deity that enables the ritualist to share, albeit briefly, in the powers and divine energy of that deity, usually for the purpose of enhancing the effectiveness of a ritual or for deep communion with that deity.

The technique of Kheperu is a defining characteristic of Egyptian and Egyptian-derived magic. There are reasons to believe that it was more than a mere invocatory convention to the Egyptians and that a genuine connection with the deity invoked was both intended and achieved. Kheperu was one of the key ways the ancient Egyptians empowered their spirituality—and it is one of the most important ways we can empower our own spirituality today.

THE PHARAOH AND KHEPERU

In the beginning, it was probably only the Pharaoh who assumed divine powers through Kheperu, the earliest forms being those of powerful animals. A number of early Egyptian palettes show animals—perhaps intended to represent the ruler in the *kheper* of an animal—destroying enemies. Indeed, Egypt's earliest-recorded kings took the names of dangerous, powerful, and sacred animals such as scorpion, kite, and cobra as a way to connect with these powers.

Yet the idea that a human being could be god-like is found throughout Egyptian literature. In the Instruction for Merikare, wisdom literature from the First Intermediate Period, it is said that the deceased is "like a god" in the beyond and refers to humanity as the "likeness of God." Humankind is called the "herd of God" and is "his likeness which came forth from his flesh." A human being with great knowledge is also said to be a likeness of the Divine. Clearly, the Egyptians recognized a fundamental kinship between the human and the Divine.

Magic for All

As time went by, however, beliefs about what happened to the pharaoh after death began to be applied more broadly. Sacred texts that

had been carved on the pyramids (the Pyramid Texts) to assist the pharaoh during his journey to the land of the dead began to be written on the coffins (the Coffin Texts) of nobles, clergy, and other wealthy people to assist them. Eventually, even those who could not afford expensive mummification and ritually inscribed coffins could gain the benefits of the sacred texts with a portable *Book of Coming Forth by Day* written on papyrus and placed with the body. By the time of the New Kingdom, even the ordinary person was promised a "god-like omniscience" in the Otherworld.

What's more, even ordinary people employed magic, *heka*, on a regular basis. The Egyptian wisdom literature said that heka was given to human beings so that they could use it "to ward off the blow of events." Essential to the Egyptian universe, magic was inseparable from a relationship with the deities. Heka was part of religion, part of life, and part of nature. It was understood to be infused in things both divine and natural, although divine things have a greater share.

A Living Relationship with Magic

In addition to being a natural energy, magic was also a living being, a god. Therefore to truly know Heka, one had to enter into a relationship with him. The magician was not a mere technician, but a technically proficient priest or priestess; a practiced channel for the influx of the divine energy of Heka. A primordial power, Heka is the power by which the spiritual becomes manifest; thus he is the power by which the priest or priestess transforms him- or herself in order to draw spiritual forces into activity in the manifested world.

The Egyptians considered the energy of magic to have a semi-physical aspect and may have conceived of it as a field of energy that surrounded the deities, providing the power with which they maintained the natural order. As a semi-physical quantity, magic can be moved or directed. Texts also refer to Heka being eaten or swallowed, thus taking magic in is volitional; and this is another important key to the technique of Kheperu. The deity is specifically invited—even claimed—by the priest or priestess. This is why modern magic workers say they invoke, assume, take on, or draw down a god or goddess form; they *choose* and activate this particular relationship with deity.

ACTIVATING KHEPERU

In addition to having a living relationship with Heka, there are a number of ways the Egyptian priest or priestess could activate the sacred magic of Kheperu. First and foremost was through the sacred power of words and names. Many of you may already know the importance the Egyptians placed on magic names and words. This is because they believed that words and names contained the essence and energy of their subject. Even as late as the second or third century CE, Egyptians knew their own language to be the true—and most powerful—sacred language. When a priest declared that he *was* Isis or Atum, he was actually calling forth the power of Isis or Atum.

The Egyptian would also identify him or herself with the deity by telling the story of the god or goddess or by relating her or his epithets as in this from the Coffin texts:

> I *am the soul of Shu the self-created god, I have come into being from the flesh of the self-created god. I am the soul of Shu, the god invisible of shape, I have come into being from the flesh of the self-created god, I am merged in the god. I have become he.*

In the rest of this spell, the priest spends time making statements that identify him with Shu. He tells the full myth of Shu, and beautifully ends the formula with the words:

> I *am invisible of shape, I am merged in the Sunshine-god.*

I have no doubt that if you worked this spell today—as written and while in the proper frame of mind—you could indeed assume the god-form or draw down Shu.

The proper frame of mind is, however, crucial. The ordinary consciousness of the priestess must be expanded in order to contact the energy of the deity invoked. She must cultivate a state of mind that is larger than her subjective self. Jeremy Naydler, author of *Temple of the Cosmos*, writes:

> ... in various magical situations a person might identify with a transpersonal energy, or god, to such an extent that their psyche became wholly absorbed into this transpersonal power. They

were no longer themselves but experienced themselves as a god and were, or could be, so experienced by others.

The Egyptian seeking this expanded state might employ sacred images along with the magical words. The priest or priestess could participate in divine energy by wearing a mask or using ritual gestures, thus becoming a sacred image her- or himself. Depictions of priests wearing Anubis masks are known and examples of the masks themselves have been found. A mask obscures the identity, outwardly enabling the priest to become an image of the deity, and inwardly to identify more fully with him. He may also have prepared himself on a psychic and energetic level: "I have come into you, having opened up my head and aroused my body," say the Coffin Texts.

Visualization is another possibility. A formula from the Book of Coming Forth by Day identifies the deceased with Re, quality by quality, easily allowing for visualization:

His *sun disk is your sun disk.*
His *rays are your rays.*
His *crown is your crown.*
His *greatness is your greatness.*
His *appearings are your appearings.*
His *beauty is your beauty.*
His *majesty is your majesty.*
His *savor is your savor.*
His *extent is your extent.*
His *seat is your seat.*
His *throne is your throne.*
His *heritage is your heritage.*
His *panoply is your panoply.*
His *destiny is your destiny.*
His *West is your West.*

His goods are your goods.
His wisdom is your wisdom.
His distinction is your distinction.

He who would protect himself does indeed protect himself—
and vice versa.

Once the Kheper is assumed, the Coffin Texts tell us, the deity is
perceived within: "Hail to you, Khopri [a solar god of transforma-
tion] within my body . . ."

Kheperu and Communion

The Egyptians employed the technique of Kheperu to increase heka
for a good outcome after death, for protection, for accomplishment
of a variety of tasks, such as healing, as well as the usual human reasons of gaining love and money. They may also have used it for ritual
theater and to enable priests to give oracles as the deity. But in addition to these uses, it is also possible that the ancients used Kheperu
as many of us do today—for communion with the Divine. The Book
of the Dead says:

> I will go into the moon-god, so that he may speak to me, that the
> followers of the gods may speak to me, that the sun may speak
> to me, that the sun-folk may speak to me.

Putting on the Cloak of the Great Lady

Under its various names, many modern magical practitioners—
from Hermetic theurgists and other ceremonial magicians who assume a god form to Wiccans who draw down the moon—use the
ancient Egyptian technique I have called Kheperu. Most commonly,
it is used in ritual so that the ritual actions one takes are informed by
the energy of the deity invoked. Kheperu enables us to tap into an

energy source greater than our own psychic powers to aid in accomplishing the purpose of the ritual. It is a step beyond reaching out in prayer because it offers the opportunity to take an active part in creating a path—through oneself—into which the immanent divine energy may be drawn. When properly done, this ancient technique puts us in touch with a deeper wisdom that will serve us as guide in any act of magic, mundane or spiritual. It means no more—and no less—than placing the divine part of the self in contact with a greater divine power. The potential that this offers for spiritual development, as well as for spell-working, is immense.

Like the ancient Egyptian who "put on the cloak of the Great Lady" and became the Great Lady Hathor, a modern witch can invoke her goddess and become the image of the goddess. If she succeeds in doing this, she will certainly know it—for the feeling is unlike any normal state of consciousness. She may feel as if her body, soul, mind, and spirit have tapped into a stream of energy coming from outside herself, a stream which extends beyond the physical and touches invisible realms. She may perceive herself as enormous, towering over the Earth or suspended in space. She may have a feeling of expansion in her heart or little rushes or spasms of energy throughout her body similar to the *kriyas* that occur in some forms of yoga. She will without doubt feel the shimmering presence of the goddesses and may participate in the emotions that are a part of that goddess' nature.

She will also discover that true divine contact, though very powerful, is humbling and does not idly flatter the ego. She may come to believe that the goddesses and gods participate in our taking on of their Kheperu not merely because of sacred names or words or images, but because of their divine love for us. She will see that when we expend our effort to reach out to the Divine, the goddesses and gods will in turn stretch out their hands to us, guiding us, assisting us in our magic, and most importantly, helping us grow spiritually.

M. Isidora Forrest *has been a devotee of the goddess Isis for more than twenty years and a Maenad priestess of the Dionysos for over ten years. She is the author of* Isis Magic: Cultivating a Relationship with the Goddess of 10,000 Names *and* Offering to Isis: Knowing the Goddess through Her Sacred Symbols. *She has also contributed to a number of anthologies. Her articles include:* "Divination in the Græco-Egyptian Magical Papyri" *in Llewellyn's* Golden Dawn Journal, Book I; "The Equilibration of Jehovah" *in* Golden Dawn Journal, Book II; *and* "The Hermetic Isis" *in* Golden Dawn Journal, Book III. *She and her husband, Adam Forrest, established the Hermetic Fellowship in Portland, Oregon, for study, discussion, and ritual in the Western Esoteric Tradition.*

Illustrator: Paul Hoffman

Personal Myths

Lupa

Hey! Did you know that I'm a dancing, white-furred, werewolf shaman who talks to trees and streams? And when I wave this shiny stick around, or beat on this drum, I can make spirits show up? Really! You don't believe me? Well, I am just telling a story . . . a very important one! What I am telling are my personal myths.

What is Personal Mythology?

People are storytellers. We are not content with the barebones facts of the world we live in, its inhabitants, and ourselves, though the facts are important. Instead, we embellish the physical reality we encounter with legends, tales, and myths. Even though these stories may only have a bare resemblance to physical reality, we still hold on to them as dearly as any objective truth. Why?

We are creatures imbued with the desire for meaning. The creation of myth serves a deep-seated need in the human psyche to assign importance to select portions of what we experience. This needn't be limited to the fantastic. Even the way we recount something that happened to us on a given day can be told in such a way as to give it great meaning; over time, these tales become a part of our personal mythology, the story we tell about ourselves.

Never heard of personal mythology? Don't feel bad; most people, Pagan or otherwise, are only familiar with cultural mythology, the stories that are shared by an entire people—and often may have nothing whatsoever to do with the members of the culture as individuals. Yet in modern American culture, and to an extent in some cultures that America has had a lot of cultural interchange with, the emphasis has shifted from being part of a cohesive, culturally-identified group toward the ascendance of the individual.

In fact, some American Pagans may feel that we really have no cultural mythology to speak of. Sure, we have Paul Bunyan, and Pecos Bill, but these don't seem to compare to the mythologies that are found in other cultures, such as ancient Greek, Norse, Egyptian, and other well-known (and not so well-known) cultural mythologies. The dominant religion in America is Christianity in its various denominations, which most Pagans don't feel the need to adhere to, even if Christian mythos does permeate American culture in numerous subtle ways. Our diversity is healthy, but one of the downfalls is that it may leave some of us feeling a bit rootless, culturally speaking.

Because we have such an emphasis on the individual in this culture, it only seems natural that we would look within to find substitutes for that which we feel we lack outside of ourselves. While personal mythology shouldn't be seen as a complete replacement for cultural mythology (and vice versa), it can be an exceedingly important meaning-making tool.

The Source of Meaning

We encounter numerous stimuli in our everyday life through our senses. Some of these stimuli affect us more than others, often to the point where we feel the need to share that enhanced effect with others. When we communicate what is special or otherwise outstanding about something, we imbue it with meaning. Granted, all animals have ways of recognizing what is most important—food, water, shelter, mates, and so forth. But due to our particularly developed brains, our recognition is more elaborate.

Meaning gives us a way to separate the things that we find most important from everything else. Furthermore, meaning-making activities can enhance the qualities of what has meaning to us through storytelling, ritual, and other "special" activities. When we tell nature-based myths, we are saying that the phenomena described in the myths, often metaphorically, are to be noticed and valued.

Additionally, we are a creative species. To put things very basically, meaning-making is a right-brain activity, and allows the part of our mind that speaks in symbols and metaphors and abstracts to be able to participate more fully in our experiences and our understanding thereof. We generally find these creative processes to be enjoyable, encouraging us to engage in them again.

Personal Mythology in NeoPaganism

NeoPaganism has developed a mythology of its own over the years. Heavily influenced by Wicca, a somewhat generic mythos based in fertility and nature has arisen; it includes various concepts, such as a more Western interpretation of reincarnation, chakras, and varying degrees of polytheism. It also relies quite a bit on archetypes—the Maiden, Mother, and Crone, and so forth (even if not all Pagans subscribe to such soft polytheism). Much of the collective mythology of neoPaganism (as a general movement) can be adopted by the individual for personal mythological purposes.

Take archetypes, for example. Leaving aside the discussion of whether deities are archetypal in nature or not, archetypes may be used in personal mythology to create a "magical self," or image of the self, as a spiritual, magical person. While it may be based in physical reality, in who you are right now, it can also draw upon the goals you have for yourself in your spiritual and/or magical practice.

For instance, some people may align themselves with the archetype of the Warrior, or the Healer, or the Shaman. These are not the sum total of everything that it is to be a warrior or healer or shaman, and may not even necessarily closely resemble any physical cultural manifestation of such a role. Yet thinking of yourself as Warrior or Healer or Shaman can help you to focus on your goal of developing a more detailed spiritual and/or magical path.

Personal mythology in Paganism needn't even be so dramatic as that. Whenever we enact rituals, we're telling stories in that moment. No longer are we people dressed in strange costumes waving fancy sticks and shiny knives and dancing in circles around campfires. Instead, we are in a place and time where we touch the sacred and divine, where our wands and ritual blades guide spirits and energies in a sacred space centered around the life-giving fire.

The danger involved, of course, is letting the map take the place of the territory. While not all Pagans are gamers, it can be easy to let your image of yourself become less like a symbol of your ideal self, and more like a role-playing game character. Don't let your imagined ideas of what a "shaman" does take the place of actually researching what shamans in various cultures do. In the same way, be aware that while a ritual you participate in may be an incredible experience, it is (as Hakim Bey says) a "temporary autonomous zone," and there are very good reasons to ground yourself afterward. Personal mythology can be useful, but don't let it completely replace your attachment to physical reality.

That being said, you shouldn't be afraid of letting your personal mythology get too crazy, just so long as you take it for what it is: a story that is based on the physical you.

How to Tell Your Story

The best place to start is your everyday life—what most people would think of as your biography, if you were asked to share yours. Sadly, many people think they live boring lives. They get up, go to work or school, come home, spend a few hours online or in front of the television—in other words, they spend most of their waking lives in routines. Yet it's the things that break the routine that are often the most interesting. And that's where the storytelling really begins.

For example, a few years ago I worked as a utility meter reader. It was my job to hunt down gas meters in the rural areas south of Pittsburgh, Pennsylvania. You'd think this would be an incredibly tedious job, and many times it was. Most of the time I simply drove from farm to farm, going to the same meters in two-month cycles. But there would be moments that were beautiful, terrifying, or humorous. Like the time I very nearly tripped over a week-old white-tail fawn in the middle of a field. Or when I lost a staredown with a bull that decided a particular meter was his (and I wasn't about to dispute that assertion!). Or the morning I went out after it snowed, with the sun just coming over the hills, turning everything into a brilliant, silent retreat from the noise of the city. In fact, some of the best stories I have came from the year-and-a-few-months I worked as a meter reader.

There are also stories about ourselves that we may not think are all that great, but that someone else may find absolutely fascinating. I don't think it's all that spectacular that I was an Army brat, yet there are people for whom that must mean I was a traveler from an early age. I also get a lot of comments on my blog when I post about my garden, especially when I add pictures. These are pretty routine things for me, but to some people, they're some of the best stories I have.

You might try writing a basic biography about yourself. Or if you spend a good deal of time online, especially on social networking sites like Facebook, LiveJournal, or MySpace, you've probably been tagged for at least a few biographical memes. If you're not a computer person, you might try recording your biography on tape. Or get together with some friends and trade self-stories. Even if you have no audience at all, pretend that you do, and that you need to tell as much as you can, starting from the beginning, or with a specific topic such as hobbies, occupations, or childhood memories.

Adding to the Myth

Hopefully, by now you've already seen that you do have some very true stories to tell about yourself. But what else is there? Your imagination is one very important component of who you are and how you view yourself. Have you ever daydreamed about being someone or something else? That's a part of the story you tell about yourself, too. It may not be literally true (at least right now) but it still points out some important things about who you are and what you would like to be capable of. The "could be" is as important as the "is" in many cases.

One thing you want to avoid is escapism. Have you ever read the story "The Secret Life of Walter Mitty" by James Thurber? The title character is a typically Thurber-esque male character, rather inept and doddering. His movements are corralled by a domineering wife, and people in his town (if you'll forgive me tossing in a bit of Rodney Dangerfield, too) don't give him "no respect." To escape this, he spends his time weaving elaborate fantasy lives, from surgeon to fighter pilot. Fantasies are no problem in and of themselves, but when they're used to avoid reality, there's something wrong with the reality that needs to be addressed. In the same way,

A quick note regarding imagination: imagination doesn't necessarily mean "not real." Unfortunately, it's generally used to refer to imaginary things, like children's make-believe.

make sure that when you're assessing your imaginative life you pay attention to how you value it compared to your "real" life.

Bridging the imaginary and the real is the magical self. Not everyone who has such a self-image is a magic-worker, but the principle is the same. The magical self is the self-image that involves a combination of who you are in physical life with who you imagine yourself to be. A quick note regarding imagination: imagination doesn't necessarily mean "not real." Unfortunately, it's generally used to refer to imaginary things like children's make-believe. Yet imagination is also integral to everything from inventing new technology to planning out a trip. And it's crucial to successful magical practice and interactions with spiritual beings. Just because something is imaginary doesn't mean it's "all made up." (A quick book recommendation for you: Patrick Harpur's *Daimonic Reality* is a lovely, if dense, treatment of imagination as more than "just made-up.")

As I mentioned earlier, the magical self can draw on archetypes for its basic form. The details, of course, are yours to personalize. You may already know what you resonate with. If you're not sure, though, look at not only how you view yourself in your daydreaming, but what sorts of spiritual and magical practices you lean toward. If you were to write a story about another person who did the same kinds of things, how would you describe them? Don't think about yourself; you want to distance yourself enough that you don't feel self-conscious. You can write up a basic character description, or entire stories if you like (again keeping in mind the difference between your life and that of the not-you-but-close character you're creating).

> **Bridging the imaginary and the real is the magical self. Not everyone who has such a self-image is a magic-worker, but the principle is the same.**

Once you have a decent idea of your magical self, look at how that carries over into your life and your practice. How close are you to your ideal? What could you do to get closer? What's simply not realistic? (I'm thinking throwing fireballs counts for that last one.)

Additionally, how do you see yourself when you're performing a ritual? Are you different from how you are in other settings? If so, how? How do you approach the spirits and other beings you may work with? Why do you use the ritual trappings that you do? What is the complete picture created by you, the spirits, the ritual tools and adornments, and the rituals themselves?

These are just a few of the ways you can start telling your own story. But what do you do with it once you have it?

The Personal Mythology in Practice

Probably one of the most important functions of personal mythology is being able to look at yourself on multiple levels, as well as sharing that with others, if you so choose. For the most part, people only really think of themselves in the context of their everyday, mundane lives. Yet there's so much more to a person than that! Personal mythology allows us to take the everyday and integrate it with the rest of ourselves without letting any one part overrun the rest.

Additionally, for the Pagan, personal mythology can inspire growth and development in one's spiritual and magical practice. I'm essentially developing a neoshamanic practice from scratch that includes rituals, tools, and even the basic cosmology. My personal mythology has helped me to understand not only why shamanism is important to me and what areas of my life tie into it, it also gives me a sort of blueprint—infinitely updateable—to further design my practice by. I have an image of myself-as-shaman that I want to cultivate, and while image is far from being everything, it does provide an idealized goal to work toward. I still have to put in the hard work, but just as we like to choose aesthetically pleasing ritual tools to help motivate us in actual ritual, so the magical self can motivate us toward growing as individuals. Those who get stuck on only developing the magical self-image are similar to those who have ritual tools only for display—they're missing the point entirely.

Beyond this point, it's all up to you where you go with your own story. I recommend that no matter what else you do, take time to not only appreciate where you've been and what you've done—no matter how "boring" it may seem—but to also look toward a future where, more than ever, you are an active creator and participant in the story that is your life.

Lupa *is a Pagan and (neo)shaman living in Portland, Oregon, with her husband, Taylor Ellwood. She is currently working on a master's degree in counseling psychology with an emphasis on ecopsychology. She is also the author and editor of several (controversial!) books on Pagan and occult topics, an avid environmentalist and sustainability geek, and a bibliophile.*

Illustrator: Bri Hermanson

Looking Back at the New Age of Witchcraft

Kimberly Sherman-Cook

As we witches, Pagans, heathens, and Wiccans venture forth into the unknown of another new year, I am struck by the notion that we are also in another decade. It has become a strong belief of mine that we can only see our path ahead by reflecting on and learning from where we have been. With that in mind, I took a look back at my own past and the beginnings of my training. I paused to reflect on how much our religion has evolved, even in the seventeen years I have been practicing witchcraft.

It was not long ago that witchcraft was the shining child of promise that heralded in a new era for those of us who wanted something other than what mainstream religions have to offer. It wasn't all that long ago that a witch was only a "true" witch if he or she had been initiated into a coven. Today, solitary witches have become the new way of our religion, while covens have become all but obsolete. All of this leads to questions like: How did we get here? Where did all of this information come from, and what can we expect in the future?

During the early years in the resurgence of Paganism, the terms *occult* and *witchcraft* were scarcely mentioned, never mind discussed openly, in public. In the late 1800s and early 1900s, our predecessors would not have dared perform a public ritual in a local park or downtown square. And many of those who practiced occult traditions attended church on Sunday and kept a very low profile with regard to their extracurricular activities, and few, if any, occult authors published works. Few people talked openly about witchcraft or Paganism the way we do today. On the surface the world probably seemed much like the movie *Pleasantville*. Underneath that calm surface, however, the womb of a new age was swelling, churning, and growing.

Up until the 1800s fraternal orders, secret societies, and individual families were the ones who maintained occult knowledge and passed this information down to subsequent generations. Then in the late 1800s, something interesting started to happen. The womb of the occult became heavy with new life, ideas, thoughts, and energy. People such as Eliphas Lévi (Alphonse Louis Constant), Charles Godfrey Leland, Margret Murray, and Aleister Crowley began to publish occult works, which sometimes made public the secrets earlier groups had protected. They based their works on earlier theories and speculation, on older texts, and on their own research. The momentum that began with their work has lasted more than one hundred years.

During the late 1940s, we were just emerging from the Great Depression and World War II. Europeans seemed to turn a blind eye to people like Crowley, and the new emergence of occult societies simmered back down—at least on the surface. The story of the rebirth of witchcraft may have ended here as a footnote in history books except for one important event. In 1951, the witchcraft laws of England were repealed. This set the stage for what was soon to become the explosion of the neoPagan movement. Suddenly witches and their covens were everywhere. People like Gerald Gardner, Doreen Valiente, Alex and Maxine Sanders, Janet and Stewart Farrar, and Raymond Buckland became the new voices of witchcraft, and ultimately they would change the map of the neoPagan movement forever.

Throughout the 1960s, 1970s, and 1980s, in both Europe and the United States, there was a strong resurgence of both Paganism and witchcraft. This was largely made possible because of technological advancements and the media. With the rise in media coverage and the seemingly odd interest of reporters in witchcraft, it was now being publicized everywhere. Books were being written and published yearly, and when combined with a greater ability to print and ship things globally, it is easy to see why there was the rise in the number of occult authors. The Pagan movement continued to make its way into the mainstream.

The world itself seemed to grow smaller as Paganism grew larger and more widespread. As news traveled ever more quickly, people could no longer turn away and ignore what was happening. Witches were alive and well, Paganism was making a comeback, and suddenly people were coming out of the broom closet to reclaim the right to practice the traditions of magick. Many Pagans during this time still lived a double life, keeping secret their involvement with a coven. If word got out, these people sometimes lost their jobs and family ties, and some were even ridiculed by their communities.

Therefore, those within the coven would take oaths of secrecy to keep safe the practices that they were taught. In addition to protecting the coven, this was done because of a long-held belief that those who were not initiated should not have access to the coven's activities. So even though the neoPagan religious movement had come far, there were still very real dangers that people faced and in some places still face today.

As more and more people joined the new movement of Paganism, covens became more plentiful and the numbers of people who practiced Paganism grew. By the late 1970s, neoPaganism had largely

Aleister Crowley

replaced the word witchcraft, because it was considered a less negative term than the latter. Witchcraft had also finally succeeded in penetrating the United States and other areas of the globe. It was clear by now that this new religion was not only NOT going away, it was spreading like wildfire.

Today, people like Maxine Sanders and Janet Farrar are considered the elders of our faith not simply because of age, but because of their experience and how they conduct themselves. And many new occult authors, including myself, have been inspired by their poetry, prose, theories, stories, and instructional books.

The craze did settle down as the media began to lose interest, and what was once new had become commonplace. The original materials set down by Gardner, Valiente, the Farrars, and Buckland continue to serve us today. My hope is that they will not be forgotten and that they will continue to enrich our understanding of this newly forming religious practice for a great many years to come. Though this was the birth and evolution of a New Age movement that we now lovingly refer to as neoPaganism, our story doesn't quite end there.

As we pushed forward in the early 1980s and 1990s, which is my generation, occult works became more common, yet it was still difficult to find books on Paganism and the occult in your average book store. The few books that were easily accessible in the New Age or World Religion sections were mostly entertainment-style, fortune-telling books rather than occult teachings. This trend would continue into the first decade of the twenty-first century, with a few notable exceptions.

During the 1980s and 1990s, Laurie Cabot (from Salem, Massachusetts) was leaving her mark in the world of witchcraft. Cabot was dubbed by Governor Dukakis in 1977 the "Official Witch of Salem." She did for Salem, Massachusetts, what Walt Disney did for Disneyland. Salem once again became a popular place to visit, both for its history and for the chance to gawk at its witches. Cabot (and some-times other members of her coven) made appearances on television and with the media, which furthered the national media's attention to Salem. During the height of her work, Cabot was even featured in *National Geographic Magazine*.

As a teenage witch growing up in Massachusetts, I was ecstatic when one of my class projects, which involved reading *The Scarlet Letter*, included a trip to Salem. As soon as it was possible, my best friend and I snuck off and checked out the local witch shops instead of visiting the historical sites we were supposed to see. Our insatiable teenaged curiosity led us into the shop that Laurie was said to own at the time, Crow Haven Corner. That was to be the first time I met the woman known as Salem's Official Witch. Since then Laurie and I have met on several occasions, and though I am sure she would scarcely remember me, she has left a lasting impression.

Curious Pagans, like myself, who lived outside of the large cities had few opportunities to find a local coven or group to train with. The Internet was still new, and although it was growing rapidly, it did not hold the vast amounts of information and online groups that it does today. Still, determination and luck were often enough to help us find or order books to study and learn from as we practiced on our own.

By the late 1990s, access to books by Silver RavenWolf, Ray Buckland, Gerina Dunwich, Edain McCoy, Scott Cunningham, Dan and Pauline Campanelli, and many others became easier as more books appeared on the shelves of local book stores. The time of scrounging for information was ending as more was now essentially at "the tip of your wand." The new Paganism authors provided an even wider range of information and gave rise to the trend of solitary practice. For virtually the first time ever, people were able to train themselves from the comfort of their homes without having to relocate or travel great distances to find a coven.

The only drawback to this form of training was that the larger community still considered solitary practitioners uninitiated witches. But neoPagan religious practices were growing faster than ever—definitely faster than a coven-centered community could support. The once hard and fast rules of initiated and uninitiated began to break down. And even though many witches still sought out a coven from which to be trained, many more of us joined the growing ranks of solitary practitioners.

As fewer traditional covens were set up and more and more à la carte teachings became the norm, people have had to make up their own minds about what, when, and how to follow the Pagan path. The uninitiated witch and Wiccan became the new way within the community and the coven structure began to take a back seat. Solitary witches were forming loosely based groups or not associating with a specific form of community at all. They were no longer concerned with being associated with a lineage or even with a tradition. Instead, they were interested in what Wicca and witchcraft had to offer them individually.

A majority of the witches I speak with today say they have trained solitarily or with instructors who offer classes to the public. Though many of them take classes with other members of the community, most witches remain somewhat removed from the organized forms of practice that were once common, citing politics, ego trips, an unhealthy community, and other forms of abuse as the main reasons for choosing not to join organized groups.

Fortunately, the solitary witch shares equal footing with the initiated witch and does not need the support of a organized group. The community has become less interested in lineage and more interested in how well you know your craft. I believe many of us have found solace and healing in working through our training on our own, taking what is perceived as dogma out of our spirituality, and choosing, instead, to empower ourselves.

... most witches today remain somewhat removed from the organized forms of practice that were once common, citing politics, ego trips, an unhealthy community, and other forms of abuse as the main reasons for choosing not to join organized groups ...

The recent changes in the Craft have begun to cause a new death of sorts. The religion is again shedding the older form of community and is now experiencing a rebirth and the evolution of a more loosely tied-together community than previously existed. Being a solitary, self-trained, and self-initiated witch, as well as a trained and coven-initiated witch, I can vouch for the fact that each path has both good and bad to offer. Each style of learning has a valuable place in the life of a witch.

The path of neoPaganism has grown not by the hundreds, but possibly the thousands, since 2001. A study conducted by ARIS (American Religious Identification Survey) out of Trinity college in Hartford, Connecticut, showed that new-movement religions (Wiccan, Pagan, or Spiritualist) have increased by four percent since their 1990 poll, which leads researchers to believe there may be as many as 2.8 million, if not more of us, living in and practicing our religions in the United States today. A statement on the ARIS Web site contributes to this finding by saying that this religious movement is growing faster now than it has in the previous years' surveys. This is just another testament to the fact that our new-age religion is not only alive and well, it is still emerging and blooming in its own unique way.

Evolution is painful, but it is necessary if we are to grow beyond the original vision of our foremothers and fathers. In looking back over our evolution, we can see that it has been a healthy process of give and take. I believe that with time the pendulum will once again swing back to a more organized way of practicing, not out of politics but out of our natural desire to unite and bond. I believe that we will do this while incorporating the new lessons that have been learned. I believe that the child of promise is now becoming an adult.

There are very few secrets left in the Craft. Many things that were once hidden are now available for everyone. This creates a certain sense of nostalgia and sometimes a concern for what may have been better left unsaid. In some sense, it is like handing your teenager the car keys and hoping they understand the full responsibility of how to use that power wisely. Any parent will tell you that some-

times you have to give in and let the child make the choices so that they will know the full weight of responsibility is resting squarely on their shoulders. Then you cross your fingers and hope. For myself, secrets are best kept secret or else they should never be kept at all. I personally do not keep many secrets, yet that does not diminish the mystery that is me. I feel the same is true of witchcraft; knowing does not cheapen the mystery of self-discovery. Since we are, after all, a mystery tradition, I believe we travel into this next decade with keys in hand and mystery in front of us. It will remain to be seen if we are wise enough to be responsible with the power given to us.

The mystery itself is a mystery that is all our own to discover, because that is the way of magick. Our current era will herald new witches and authors to it; it will be our own experience to explore and expand on. There will be new ideas, perspectives, and ways to do things. The community will grow, and we will continue to share our rich heritage together. It will see the rise and fall of various ways to practice the Craft and the torch will be picked up once more. It will pierce the darkness and shine its light upon us, moving us ever forward to an unknown future.

Kimberly Sherman-Cook *is a cofounder, director, and teacher at the Pagan Education Network in Massachusetts. She has been involved in magick studies for over seventeen years, and is the leader of the Raven Star Coven, which she helped establish in 2006.*

Illustrator: Rik Olson

The Lunar Calendar

September 2010 to December 2011

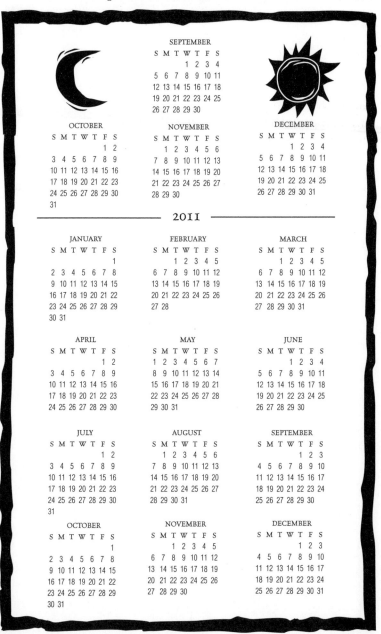

SEPTEMBER

S	M	T	W	T	F	S
			1	2	3	4
5	6	7	8	9	10	11
12	13	14	15	16	17	18
19	20	21	22	23	24	25
26	27	28	29	30		

OCTOBER

S	M	T	W	T	F	S
					1	2
3	4	5	6	7	8	9
10	11	12	13	14	15	16
17	18	19	20	21	22	23
24	25	26	27	28	29	30
31						

NOVEMBER

S	M	T	W	T	F	S
	1	2	3	4	5	6
7	8	9	10	11	12	13
14	15	16	17	18	19	20
21	22	23	24	25	26	27
28	29	30				

DECEMBER

S	M	T	W	T	F	S
			1	2	3	4
5	6	7	8	9	10	11
12	13	14	15	16	17	18
19	20	21	22	23	24	25
26	27	28	29	30	31	

2011

JANUARY

S	M	T	W	T	F	S
						1
2	3	4	5	6	7	8
9	10	11	12	13	14	15
16	17	18	19	20	21	22
23	24	25	26	27	28	29
30	31					

FEBRUARY

S	M	T	W	T	F	S
		1	2	3	4	5
6	7	8	9	10	11	12
13	14	15	16	17	18	19
20	21	22	23	24	25	26
27	28					

MARCH

S	M	T	W	T	F	S
		1	2	3	4	5
6	7	8	9	10	11	12
13	14	15	16	17	18	19
20	21	22	23	24	25	26
27	28	29	30	31		

APRIL

S	M	T	W	T	F	S
					1	2
3	4	5	6	7	8	9
10	11	12	13	14	15	16
17	18	19	20	21	22	23
24	25	26	27	28	29	30

MAY

S	M	T	W	T	F	S
1	2	3	4	5	6	7
8	9	10	11	12	13	14
15	16	17	18	19	20	21
22	23	24	25	26	27	28
29	30	31				

JUNE

S	M	T	W	T	F	S
			1	2	3	4
5	6	7	8	9	10	11
12	13	14	15	16	17	18
19	20	21	22	23	24	25
26	27	28	29	30		

JULY

S	M	T	W	T	F	S
					1	2
3	4	5	6	7	8	9
10	11	12	13	14	15	16
17	18	19	20	21	22	23
24	25	26	27	28	29	30
31						

AUGUST

S	M	T	W	T	F	S
	1	2	3	4	5	6
7	8	9	10	11	12	13
14	15	16	17	18	19	20
21	22	23	24	25	26	27
28	29	30	31			

SEPTEMBER

S	M	T	W	T	F	S
				1	2	3
4	5	6	7	8	9	10
11	12	13	14	15	16	17
18	19	20	21	22	23	24
25	26	27	28	29	30	

OCTOBER

S	M	T	W	T	F	S
						1
2	3	4	5	6	7	8
9	10	11	12	13	14	15
16	17	18	19	20	21	22
23	24	25	26	27	28	29
30	31					

NOVEMBER

S	M	T	W	T	F	S
		1	2	3	4	5
6	7	8	9	10	11	12
13	14	15	16	17	18	19
20	21	22	23	24	25	26
27	28	29	30			

DECEMBER

S	M	T	W	T	F	S
				1	2	3
4	5	6	7	8	9	10
11	12	13	14	15	16	17
18	19	20	21	22	23	24
25	26	27	28	29	30	31

The hours of sunlight grow short as Mabon, the second harvest, approaches. Characterized by the dwindling of light and life, and the struggle for balance, Mabon is the momentary equality of day and night, light and dark.

Before the balance tips over into darkness, consciously endeavor to store the brilliance of the Sun to take with you into the winter months. Make jam from late raspberries, dig potatoes to store in the root cellar, pick apples to eat or make into sauce, and gather late-summer flowers to bring some of their brilliance inside.

Calendula officinalis, a bright yellow to orange daisy-like beauty, is renowned as a treatment for skin disorders. Also called pot marigold, it has bactericide, antiseptic, and anti-inflammatory qualities. An edible flower, the petals contain powerful antioxidants. All these beneficial qualities come from soaking up the rays of the Sun.

As one of the last flowers to die after the first frost, calendula is an available source of brilliance. Add the bright petals to salad, or make calendula-infused oils for culinary and cosmetic use.

Symbolic of sunlight, calendula's spiritual qualities contribute to spells for protection, prosperity, and self-confidence. Place calendula flowers or petals on your altar, incanting: "Pretty petals, orange and bright, fill my future with abundant light." Sprinkle the petals in your bath water, and as you submerge yourself, affirm: "Protection, safety, balance and power, cloak me in your magic power." Envision the brilliance of the petals filling you and say: "Within me there is always light, in winter's dark my spirit is bright."

Be brilliantly blessed.

~Dallas Jennifer Cobb

2010
SEPTEMBER

SU	M	TU	W	TH	F	SA
			1	2	3	4
5	6	7	8 ● 6:30 am	9	10	11
	Labor Day					
12	13	14	15	16	17	18
19	20	21	22	23 ☺ Harvest Moon, 5:17am Mabon/ Fall Equinox	24	25
26	27	28	29	30		

New and Full Moon dates are shown in Eastern Time. You must adjust
the time (and date) for your time zone.

Autumn is a season of repose, a time when Mother Earth winds down and prepares for winter's restorative nap. One of the most beautiful—and visible—signs of this change is all around us in the changing colors of autumn leaves.

In the warm spring and summer months, the process of photosynthesis produces sugar in the leaves during the long days; this creates chlorophyll, which gives the leaves their typical green color. During the warm summer nights, the sugars are absorbed into each tree's cells to fuel its energy processes. But once fall comes, the nights grow cool and the dropping temperature prevents trees from absorbing the sugars. A chemical reaction causes the retained sugars to be broken down into compounds known as anthocyanins, which occur in brilliant shades of red, orange, and purple.

With the cooler nights of autumn, photosynthesis and sugar absorption slow way down. The leaves produce less chlorophyll, and the anthocyanins that are normally cloaked by chlorophyll become visible, causing deciduous trees to take on fall colors of red, gold, and orange. Eventually, photosynthesis stops altogether; the leaves drop and winter begins.

Use these ideas magickally to think about your approach to autumn and winter. What changes do you experience as the winter months approach? What hidden talents or beauties become visible as you enter the season of repose? Winter is a lovely time, a long nap that can be used to catch up on reading, work on tool craft, study divination, or engage in any type of focused magickal study. It's a perfect time for making plans, preparing for the fresh, green rebirth of spring.

~Susan Pesznecker

2010
OCTOBER

SU	M	TU	W	TH	F	SA
					1	2
3	4	5	6	7 ● 2:45 pm	8	9
10	11 *Columbus Day (observed)*	12	13	14	15	16
17	18	19	20	21	22 ☺ *Blood Moon, 9:37 pm*	23
24	25	26	27	28	29	30
31 *Samhain/ Halloween*						

Whenever the moon and stars are set, whenever the wind is high,
All night long in the dark and wet, a man goes riding by.
Late in the night when the fires are out,
Why does he gallop and gallop about?
~Robert Louis Stevenson

My favorite magical comfort food is chicken barley soup. The soup is light but filling. Made with fresh vegetables and chicken, it is a wonderful late fall or early winter meal. Start the soup early in the day and serve with lots of crusty bread and butter.

~Boudica

Chicken Barley Soup

1 cup uncooked barley
1 small whole chicken (skin removed)
3 large carrots, cut into quarter-inch rounds
3 large stalks of celery, cut into quarter-inch pieces
1 large onion, chopped
½ teaspoon basil, or 3 or 4 fresh leaves, chopped fine
½ teaspoon sage, or 3 or 4 fresh leaves, chopped fine
Fresh ground pepper (to taste)
Kosher salt to taste

In a large slow cooker, set on high, place barley, chicken, chopped carrots, chopped celery, and onion. Cover with water, stir occasionally, and add water to keep chicken covered. Let cook until chicken starts to falls off the bone and barley is soft (up to 2½ hours). When the chicken is done, remove the onion if you don't want it in the soup. Remove the chicken and allow to cool somewhat; remove the meat from the bones and return meat to pot. Add basil, sage, salt, and pepper to taste. Allow to sit on simmer, stirring occasionally, until everyone gets home.

Store leftover soup in a covered container in the refrigerator. Makes up to 5 servings.

2010
NOVEMBER

SU	M	TU	W	TH	F	SA
	1 All Saints' Day	2 Election Day (general)	3	4	5	6 ● 12:52 am
7 DST ends, 2 am	8	9	10	11 Veterans Day	12	13
14	15	16	17	18	19	20
21 ☺ Mourning Moon, 12:27 pm	22	23	24	25 Thanksgiving Day	26	27
28	29	30				

O Lady Moon, your horns point to the East.
Shine be increased!
O Lady Moon, your horns point to the West.
Wane, be at rest.

SAGITTARIUS

With Yule, Christmas, and Hanukkah, there is so much to celebrate in December. These versatile and tasty treats that are good for body and soul. They are suitable for people who are vegan, vegetarian, or who have celiac disease, and will make a delicious treat to share with your friends, family, and neighbors this holiday season. Holiday Hemp Suns are made from fruit and nuts, the traditional foods of Yule; and they combine the superior protein of hemp seeds with the sweet goodness of dates (not suitable for people with nut allergies). Delicious and nutritious, Holiday Hemp Suns are filled with essential fatty acids and shaped like the Sun that we celebrate this season.

~Dallas Jennifer Cobb

Holiday Hemp Suns

2 cups of pitted, dried dates
1 cup of hulled hemp seeds
1 cup of shelled walnuts
Shredded coconut (optional)
Cocoa powder (optional)

In a food processor, puree dates until smooth. Add hemp seeds and walnuts. Puree until the mixture reaches a consistent fudge-like texture. Use your hands to roll mixture into 1 inch balls; place on a plate and chill. Optional: Roll balls in shredded coconut or cocoa powder to dress them up and add to flavor. Makes approximately 32 balls.

Decorate small boxes, place several Hemp Suns inside, and tie the box with a festive ribbon.

2010
DECEMBER

SU	M	TU	W	TH	F	SA
			1	2	3	4
5 ● 12:36 pm	6	7	8	9	10	11
12	13	14	15	16	17	18
19	20	21 ☺ Long Nights Moon, 3:13 am Lunar Eclipse Yule/ Winter Solstice	22	23	24 Christmas Eve	25 Christmas Day
26	27	28	29	30	31 New Year's Eve	

Laughter is the sun that drives winter from the human face.
~Victor Hugo

Winter sets in and we remember the summer, when we had fresh vegetables and salads on our plates. I love tomatoes fresh from the garden that are topped with fresh basil and served on crusty bread. If I am at the grocery and find some fresh-on-the-vine tomatoes, I can't resist picking them up and taking them home.

Try this quick appetizer. Use tomatoes on the vine that smell like tomatoes. Use your nose to tell you they are fresh, ripe tomatoes. They are even better if you get them from the organic section of the grocery.

You also want fresh mozzarella. Fresh mozzarella should be soft, creamy, and sweet.

You will also need sweet basil. Sometimes you can find bunches of fresh basil in the stores. Otherwise, use the dried variety.

You will finish this dish with toasted crusty Italian bread and extra virgin olive oil—slightly warm is best.

Turn oven on to broil. Slice the tops off the tomatoes, and slice the cheese. Chop up the leaves of basil if you have fresh, or just sprinkle the tomatoes with basil and then top with the sliced cheese. Arrange tomatoes on a baking pan; place pan in the middle of the oven and broil until the cheese browns (not more than 15 or 20 minutes). Do not place directly under the broiler or the cheese will burn.

Cut up the tomatoes with the browned cheese and serve with the toasted bread. Dip the bread in the warm olive oil and scoop up the tomato/cheese mix, and enjoy a magical summer moment in the middle of winter!

~Boudica

2011
JANUARY

SU	M	TU	W	TH	F	SA
						1 *New Year's Day* *Kwanzaa ends*
2	3	4 ● 4:03 am Solar eclipse	5	6	7	8
9	10	11	12	13	14	15
16	17	18	19 ☺ 4:21 pm Cold Moon	20	21	22
23	24	25	26	27	28	29
30	31					

Observe constantly that all things take place by change.
~Marcus Aurelius

Love's Philosophy

The Fountains mingle with the Rivers
And the Rivers with the Oceans,
The winds of Heaven mix forever
With a sweet emotion;
Nothing in the world is single;
All things by a law divine
In one spirit meet and mingle.
Why not I with thine?

See the mountains kiss high Heaven
And the waves clasp one another;
No sister-flower would be forgiven
If it disdained its brother,
And the sunlight clasps the earth
And the moonbeams kiss the sea:
What is all this sweet work worth
If thou kiss not me?
~Percy Bysshe Shelley

2011
FEBRUARY

SU	M	TU	W	TH	F	SA
		1	2 ● 9:31 pm Imbolc/ Groundhog Day	3	4	5
6	7	8	9	10	11	12
13	14 Valentine's Day	15	16	17	18 ☺ Quickening Moon, 3:36 am	19
20	21	22	23	24	25	26
27	28					

You can't do it unless you imagine it.
~George Lucas

Many people speculate that St. Patrick's Day is actually a disguised celebration of the Spring Equinox. Today, we celebrate by wearing green clothes, eating corned beef and cabbage, drinking beer (sometimes dyed green), and dancing to lively Irish music. What's for dessert? Green cookies, of course!

St Patrick's Day Cookies

1 cup butter

¾ cup sugar

1 egg

2 to 3 drops green food coloring

1 teaspoon vanilla extract

2 cups flour

½ cup ground or finely chopped almonds

½ cup poppy seeds

¼ teaspoon salt

Green colored sugar

Cream the butter until soft. Add the sugar, egg, food coloring, and vanilla; mix well. Mix together flour, almonds, poppy seeds, and salt in a small bowl. Add to butter mixture and beat well. Divide the dough in half and form into logs; roll in green colored sugar. Wrap in waxed paper and chill for at least an hour. Preheat oven to 325°F. Slice logs about ¼-inch thick, and bake for 12 minutes or until edges start to brown. Yields about 4 dozen cookies.

~Magenta Griffith

2011
MARCH

SU	M	TU	W	TH	F	SA
		I	2	3	4 ● 3:46 pm	5
6	7	8	9	10	II	12
13 DST *begins,* *2 am*	14	15	16	17 *St. Patrick's Day*	18	19 ☺ Storm Moon, 2:10 pm
20 *Ostara/* *Spring Equinox*	21	22	23	24	25	26
27	28	29	30	31		

Beware the ides of March.
~William Shakespeare

April Fools' Day falls on the first day of this month, but we can feel it resonate through the entire thirty days if we try. No one is sure of the origins of this silly day. Various sources suggest that it started with confusion when the Gregorian calendar came into use (thus moving New Year's Day from April 1st to January 1st). Others claim it was originally the celebration of the goddess Venus on the Roman holiday of Veneralia. It is even said to be associated with the Spring Equinox, when Mother Nature herself often plays a cruel trick or two.

My favorite fool is the Fool card from the tarot. The most common representation of the Fool is that of a young man with his meager possessions hanging in a bag from the end of his staff. He is preparing to cheerfully step off the side of a cliff. How foolish indeed!

But wait—maybe not. After all, life is filled with moments that require a leap of faith. Take love, for instance. Lots of leaping there, and plenty of fools to go around. But where would we be if we didn't occasionally step off that cliff in spite of the risks?

So this April, why not resolve to be foolish? Make a list for yourself of all the dreams you put away as too crazy, too impossible, or too frightening to even try to achieve. Then, close your eyes and take a leap of faith. And maybe add a prayer to Venus—just to be on the safe side.

Happy foolishness!

~Deborah Blake

2011
APRIL

SU	M	TU	W	TH	F	SA
					1	2
					All Fools' Day	
3 ● 10:32 am	4	5	6	7	8	9
10	11	12	13	14	15	16
17 ☺ Wind Moon, 10:44 pm	18	19	20	21	22 Earth Day	23
24	25	26	27	28	29	30

The past should be a springboard, not a hammock.
~Ivern Ball

The Fair Flower of May

White coral bells
Upon a slender stalk
Lilies of the valley
Deck my garden walk
Oh don't you wish
That you might hear them ring?
That will only happen
When the fairies sing.

Lily-of-the-valley, or May flowers as it is sometimes called, is a hardy perennial. The tiny, white flowers turn yellow in late summer, and small red berries form on the plant in the fall. Though all parts of the plant are poisonous, herbalists have recommended using the plant for gout and heart ailments. The flower is also called "Our Lady's Tears" and is considered a flower of the Virgin Mary and a symbol of purity. In the Victorian age, a gift of these flowers meant sweetness, return to happiness, or "you made my life complete." In Ireland, lily-of-the-valley was called "fairy ladders" since it provided Fair Folk with ways to climb into this world to work magic and wonder. In contemporary times, this information can be regarded as interesting lore and not a prescription for use. Nevertheless, the sweet-scented flower has been used in perfumes for centuries.

As you walk the gardens in springtime and spy the tiny bells, listen for the singing of the Wee Ones and celebrate the return of spring, flowers, and happiness.

~Gail Wood

2011
MAY

SU	M	TU	W	TH	F	SA
I Beltane	2	3 ● 2:51 am	4	5	6	7
8 Mother's Day	9 Census Day (Canada)	10	11	12	13	14
15	16	17 ☺ Flower Moon, 7:09 am	18	19	20	21
22	23	24	25	26	27	28
29	30 Memorial Day (observed)	31				

Expect to have hope rekindled. Expect your prayers to be answered in wondrous ways.
The dry seasons in life do not last. The spring rains will come again.
~Sarah Ban Breathnach

My Fairy

I have a fairy by my side
Which says I must not sleep,
When once in pain I loudly cried
It said "You must not weep"
If, full of mirth, I smile and grin,
It says "You must not laugh"
When once I wished to drink some gin
It said "You must not quaff."

When once a meal I wished to taste
It said "You must not bite"
When to the wars I went in haste
It said "You must not fight."

"What may I do?" at length I cried,
Tired of the painful task.
The fairy quietly replied,
And said "You must not ask."

Moral: "You mustn't."
~Lewis Carroll

SU	M	TU	W	TH	F	SA
			I ● 5:03 pm Solar eclipse	2	3	4
5	6	7	8	9	10	11
12	13	14 Flag Day	15 ☺ Strong Sun Moon, 4:14 pm Lunar eclipse	16	17	18
19 Father's Day	20	21 Litha/ Summer Solstice	22	23	24	25
26	27	28	29	30		

How did it get so late so soon? It's night before it's afternoon.
December is here before it's June. My goodness how the time has flewn.
How did it get so late so soon?
~Dr. Seuss

Bed in Summer Poem

In winter I get up at night,
And dress by yellow candle light.
In summer quite the other way,
I have to go to bed by day.

I have to go to bed and see
The birds still hopping on the tree,
Or hear the grown-up people's feet
Still going past me in the street.

And does it not seem hard to you,
When all the sky is clear and blue,
And I should like so much to play,
To have to go to bed by day?
~Robert Louis Stevenson

2011
JULY

SU	M	TU	W	TH	F	SA
					I ● 4:54 am Solar eclipse	2
3	4 Independence Day	5	6	7	8	9
10	II	12	13	14	15 ☺ Blessing Moon, 2:40 am	16
17	18	19	20	21	22	23
24	25	26	27	28	29	30 ● 2:40 pm
31						

He was in love with life as an ant on a summer blade of grass.
~Ben Hecht

LEO

You can capture the color of a beach sunset in this chilled beverage that you and guests can enjoy on warm summer nights. This recipe has an adult-only option, but it can be made non-alcoholic and enjoyed by everyone. Use clear glasses to serve these blue and pink drinks.

~Norah Lea

Ocean-sunset Chilled Drinks

Blue raspberry drink, chilled
Grenadine or raspberry syrup
Ice cubes
Maraschino cherries
Ginger beer, chilled (ginger ale can be used)

Directions for adult version:
Fill each glass with half blue raspberry drink and half ginger beer. Then pour a teaspoon of grenadine or raspberry syrup into each glass (adding the syrup last will achieve the colored-layer effect). Drop in an ice cube and a cherry. Serve immediately.

Directions for youngster's version:
Substitute ginger ale for ginger beer.

2011
AUGUST

SU	M	TU	W	TH	F	SA
	1 *Lammas*	2	3	4	5	6
7	8	9	10	11	12	13 ☺ Corn Moon, 2:58 pm
14	15	16	17	18	19	20
21	22	24	25	26	27	28
29 ● 11:04 pm	30	31				

Summer bachelors, like summer breezes, are never as cool as they pretend to be.
~Nora Ephron

September is a time of transition. It can be easy to feel over-whelmed as we come back from summer vacations or get ready for new school year. Fortunately, September comes with a built-in reminder of balance: the equinox.

This month, write down all the big things you want to keep balanced in the coming year. You probably want to include family, work, hobbies, and spirituality, but you might also include big projects (like renovating your house) or volunteer commitments. Once you have your list, make a small token that will remind you to keep balance in your life. All you need is some ribbon or embroidery floss and maybe a few special charms or beads.

Choose a different color for each major area in your life. Pick the colors that speak to you. You might choose red for your family (for love), green for work (for prosperity), or yellow (for creative projects). Braid or knot the ribbons or floss together so that they connect and intertwine but stay balanced. (If you don't know how to braid, simple knots with space between them work well.) You can also include charms or large beads for special events that are coming in your life.

When you're done, put your token somewhere in your home that you'll see regularly, like an altar, near your bathroom mirror, or by your bed. When you feel your life is getting out of balance, spend time with your token. Let it remind you of what you value, and how all the parts of your life connect to each other. Use that reminder to help you continue to make balanced choices and find joy in all parts of your life.

~Jenett Silver

2011
SEPTEMBER

SU	M	TU	W	TH	F	SA
				1	2	3
4	5 Labor Day	6	7	8	9	10
11	12 ☺ Harvest Moon, 5:27 am	13	14	15	16	17
18	19	20	21	22	23 Mabon/ Fall Equinox	24
25	26	27 ● 7:09 am	28	29	30	

If you do not sow in the spring, you will not reap in the autumn.
~Irish Proverb

LIBRA

As you slide into darkness, why not transform some aspect of your life? Remember Cinderella? A lowly pumpkin was transformed into a stagecoach to carry the transformed Cinderella to the ball. As you transform a pumpkin into a thing of beauty, protection, and power, you can symbolically work to transform an aspect of your life with positive intention.

Identify something you want to change, maybe a self-destructive habit that needs to be replaced with something uplifting. Perhaps you eat poorly or smoke and want to supplant the negative behavior with something positive, like exercise.

Like Cinderella, a jolly, fat pumpkin can be your vehicle of transformation. Select a pumpkin from a farmer's field, grocery store, or your own garden, and do a simple spell. Carefully carve it open, envisioning what you want to excise from your life. Reach inside and grasp the gooey seeds, stating: I remove what is not wanted.

Throw the gooey stuff and seeds onto your compost pile, intoning: I compost the old to feed the new. By the time spring comes, the compost pile will have transformed into fertile soil.

Now, take a knife and decorate the pumpkin with a face or symbols representing beauty, protection, and power. As you carve, think: I transform my life, like this pumpkin, creating something good and new.

Now, place a small tealight candle inside the pumpkin, and light it, affirming: Light within burning bright, transformation is my right.

When you need to reaffirm your commitment to self-transformation, simply light a candle and symbolically relight the light of transformation within.

~Dallas Jennifer Cobb

2011
OCTOBER

SU	M	TU	W	TH	F	SA
						1
2	3	4	5	6	7	8
9	10 Columbus Day (observed)	11 ☺ Blood Moon, 10:06 pm	12	13	14	15
16	17	18	19	20	21	22
23	24	25	26 ● 3:56 pm	27	28	29
30	31 Samhain/ Halloween					

If I had a world of my own, everything would be nonsense.
Nothing would be what it is, because everything would be what it isn't.
And contrary wise, what is, it wouldn't be. And what it wouldn't be, it would. You see?
~Alice in Wonderland, 1951 MOVIE

Nightwind

Darkness like midnight from the sobbing woods
Clamours with dismal tidings of the rain,
Roaring as rivers breaking loose in floods
To spread and foam and deluge all the plain.
The cotter listens at his door again,
Half doubting whether it be floods or wind,
And through the thickening darkness looks afraid,
Thinking of roads that travel has to find
Through night's black depths in danger's garb arrayed.
And the loud glabber round the flaze soon stops
When hushed to silence by the lifted hand
Of fearing dame who hears the noise in dread
And thinks a deluge comes to drown the land;
Nor dares she go to bed until the tempest drops.

~John Clare

2011
NOVEMBER

SU	M	TU	W	TH	F	SA
		1 All Saints' Day	2	3	4	5
6 DST ends, 2 am	7	8 Election Day (general)	9	10 ☺ Mourning Moon, 3:16pm	11 Veterans Day	12
13	14	15	16	17	18	19
20	21	22	23	24 Thanksgiving Day	25 ● 1:10 am Solar eclipse	26
27	28	29	30			

We allow our ignorance to prevail upon us and make us think we can survive alone,
alone in patches, alone in groups, alone in races, even alone in genders.
~Maya Angelou

SAGITTARIUS

Deer appear in stories and myths throughout the magickal world. Known to be shy creatures, they are regarded as both solitary and herd animals. Much of their activity is nocturnal, earning them a reputation as one of the night's gentle ghosts. They're strongly associated with winter, particularly as objects of the hunt. Deer have long been an important food source during the cold months, and the male deer, or stag, remains sacred to the dark season as a symbol of the Horned God, who reigns during winter.

Deer can be found bounding through the ancient stories of Egypt, Greece, India, and much of Indo-European myth. In Celtic tradition, deer often appear as magickal beings during the Wild Hunt, where they mark entry into the faerie realm or serve as a transfigured form for otherworldly women. Celtic tradition suggests that the Winter Solstice is the time when the Sun King dies and the Holly King rises. Since the stag is a symbol of the Holly King, winter is the time for deer to come into their sacred power.

The king stag is one of the strongest of archetypal male symbols, and the old kings were often crowned with antlers, as in the Arthurian legends. In more shamanistic cultures, the medicine man would wear antlers to invoke the forest god and ensure a good hunting season for the upcoming year. The oldest-known masks found among aboriginal tribes in the United States are of deer and elk. Following these ancient guides, today's magick users revere the stag as a symbol of pride, strength, and virility, as well as a focus of consecration or purification.

~Susan Pesznecker

SU	M	TU	W	TH	F	SA
				1 ,	2	3
4	5	6	7	8	9	10 ☺ Long Night's Moon, 9:36 am Lunar eclipse
11	12	13	14	15	16	17
18	19	20	21	22 Yule/ Winter Solstice	23	24 ● 1:06 am Christmas Eve
25 Christmas Day	26	27	28	29	30	31 New Year's Eve

Self-discipline is an act of cultivation.
It requires you to connect today's actions to tomorrow's results.
~Gary Ryan Blair

Moon Void-of-Course Data for 2010

Last Aspect		New Sign	
Date	Time	Sign	New Time

JANUARY

Date	Time	Sign	New Time
1	10:43 am	1 ♌	9:41 pm
3	4:55 pm	3 ♍	9:52 pm
5	12:25 pm	5 ♎	11:58 pm
8	1:07 am	8 ♏	5:00 am
10	10:02 am	10 ♐	1:10 pm
12	9:43 pm	12 ♑	11:54 pm
15	4:02 am	15 ♒	12:17 pm
17	3:22 pm	18 ♓	1:17 am
20	1:06 am	20 ♈	1:36 pm
22	2:46 pm	22 ♉	11:39 pm
24	10:03 pm	25 ♊	6:11 am
27	1:32 am	27 ♋	9:01 am
28	11:49 pm	29 ♌	9:10 am
31	1:27 am	31 ♍	8:23 am

FEBRUARY

Date	Time	Sign	New Time
1	11:17 pm	2 ♎	8:42 am
4	4:27 am	4 ♏	11:56 am
6	11:11 am	6 ♐	7:04 pm
8	11:58 pm	9 ♑	5:43 am
11	7:39 am	11 ♒	6:24 pm
13	11:33 pm	14 ♓	7:23 am
16	9:32 am	16 ♈	7:30 pm
18	10:52 pm	19 ♉	5:55 am
21	7:15 am	21 ♊	1:47 pm
23	12:29 pm	23 ♋	6:29 pm
25	12:48 pm	25 ♌	8:08 pm
27	3:15 pm	27 ♍	7:52 pm

MARCH

Date	Time	Sign	New Time
1	12:36 pm	1 ♎	7:31 pm
3	3:43 pm	3 ♏	9:11 pm
5	11:32 pm	6 ♐	2:36 am
8	6:13 am	8 ♑	12:13 pm
10	4:59 pm	11 ♒	12:42 am
13	7:57 am	13 ♓	1:44 pm
15	8:01 pm	16 ♈	2:32 am
18	7:23 am	18 ♉	12:29 pm
20	3:41 pm	20 ♊	8:28 pm
22	9:49 pm	23 ♋	2:16 am
25	12:39 am	25 ♌	5:39 am
27	3:04 am	27 ♍	6:57 am
29	2:55 am	29 ♎	7:21 am
31	8:13 am	31 ♏	8:41 am

APRIL

Date	Time	Sign	New Time
2	8:54 am	2 ♐	12:53 pm
4	4:57 pm	4 ♑	9:07 pm
7	4:18 am	7 ♒	8:51 am
9	5:44 pm	9 ♓	9:48 pm
12	8:51 am	12 ♈	9:31 am
14	3:23 pm	14 ♉	6:55 pm
17	12:57 am	17 ♊	2:08 am
19	6:21 am	19 ♋	7:39 am
21	10:07 am	21 ♌	11:42 am
23	11:35 am	23 ♍	2:24 pm
25	2:21 pm	25 ♎	4:16 pm
27	3:45 pm	27 ♏	6:28 pm
29	8:39 pm	29 ♐	10:36 pm

MAY

Date	Time	Sign	New Time
2	4:08 am	2 ♑	6:00 am
4	3:07 pm	4 ♒	4:52 pm
7	2:36 am	7 ♓	5:34 am
9	4:12 pm	9 ♈	5:29 pm
12	12:11 am	12 ♉	2:48 am
14	8:28 am	14 ♊	9:18 am
16	1:06 pm	16 ♋	1:46 pm
18	4:35 pm	18 ♌	5:06 pm
20	7:43 pm	20 ♍	7:58 pm
22	10:34 pm	22 ♎	10:50 pm
25	12:01 am	25 ♏	2:17 am
27	7:13 am	27 ♐	7:15 am
29	12:40 pm	29 ♑	2:44 pm
31	11:41 pm	6/1 ♒	1:08 am

JUNE

Date	Time	Sign	New Time
5/31	11:41 pm	1 ♒	1:08 am
3	10:56 am	3 ♓	1:34 pm
6	1:49 am	6 ♈	1:50 am
8	9:13 am	8 ♉	11:41 am
10	3:50 pm	10 ♊	6:11 pm
12	7:35 pm	12 ♋	9:50 pm
14	8:38 pm	14 ♌	11:54 pm
16	11:24 pm	17 ♍	1:41 am
19	1:04 am	19 ♎	4:13 am
21	5:44 am	21 ♏	8:14 am
23	11:32 am	23 ♐	2:10 pm
25	7:33 pm	25 ♑	10:21 pm
28	5:56 am	28 ♒	8:52 am
30	6:03 pm	30 ♓	9:10 am

JULY

Date	Time	Sign	New Time
3	7:17 am	3 ♈	9:44 am
5	5:24 pm	5 ♉	8:29 pm
8	2:10 am	8 ♊	3:51 am
10	6:17 am	10 ♋	7:38 am
12	7:48 am	12 ♌	8:53 am
14	6:23 am	14 ♍	9:15 am
16	9:46 am	16 ♎	10:24 am
18	10:26 am	18 ♏	1:42 pm
20	7:43 pm	20 ♐	7:58 pm
23	12:50 am	23 ♑	4:39 am
25	10:20 am	25 ♒	3:38 pm
27	11:46 pm	28 ♓	4:00 am
29	11:44 pm	30 ♈	4:42 pm

AUGUST

Date	Time	Sign	New Time
1	11:54 pm	2 ♉	4:13 am
4	8:44 am	4 ♊	12:54 pm
6	5:22 pm	6 ♋	5:50 pm
7	2:46 pm	8 ♌	7:23 pm
10	3:10 pm	10 ♍	7:01 pm
11	8:04 pm	12 ♎	6:43 pm
14	4:06 pm	14 ♏	8:26 pm
17	1:24 am	17 ♐	1:34 am
19	9:58 am	19 ♑	10:17 am
21	9:08 pm	21 ♒	9:37 pm
24	4:29 am	24 ♓	10:11 am
26	10:00 pm	26 ♈	10:49 pm
29	4:47 am	29 ♉	10:35 am
31	7:13 pm	31 ♊	8:19 pm

SEPTEMBER

Date	Time	Sign	New Time
3	1:40 am	3 ♋	2:50 am
5	4:31 am	5 ♌	5:45 am
7	4:17 am	7 ♍	5:53 am
9	4:59 am	9 ♎	5:01 am
11	1:16 am	11 ♏	5:21 am
13	7:53 am	13 ♐	8:52 am
15	2:52 pm	15 ♑	4:30 pm
18	1:13 am	18 ♒	3:35 am
20	9:09 am	20 ♓	4:15 pm
23	1:52 am	23 ♈	4:47 am
25	9:12 am	25 ♉	4:17 pm
27	11:03 pm	28 ♊	2:10 am
30	6:37 am	30 ♋	9:46 am

OCTOBER

Date	Time	Sign	New Time
2	11:21 am	2 ♌	2:21 am
4	9:52 am	4 ♍	4:00 am
6	12:43 pm	6 ♎	3:52 pm
8	9:38 am	8 ♏	3:52 pm
10	2:27 pm	10 ♐	6:09 pm
12	8:08 pm	13 ♑	12:17 am
15	5:49 am	15 ♒	10:04 am
17	2:49 pm	17 ♓	10:52 pm
20	6:25 am	20 ♈	11:23 am
22	9:37 pm	22 ♉	10:30 pm
25	3:49 am	25 ♊	7:47 am
27	10:19 am	27 ♋	3:14 pm
29	3:48 pm	29 ♌	8:39 pm
31	5:01 pm	31 ♍	11:51 pm

NOVEMBER

Date	Time	Sign	New Time
2	8:36 pm	3 ♎	1:19 am
4	7:34 pm	5 ♏	2:16 am
6	11:44 pm	7 ♐	3:28 am
9	7:35 am	9 ♑	8:37 am
11	2:57 pm	11 ♒	5:32 pm
14	1:33 am	14 ♓	5:24 am
16	11:37 am	16 ♈	5:59 pm
19	12:33 am	19 ♉	5:04 am
21	12:27 pm	21 ♊	1:46 pm
23	4:56 pm	23 ♋	8:14 pm
25	10:44 pm	26 ♌	1:01 am
28	3:30 am	28 ♍	4:34 am
30	6:17 am	30 ♎	7:15 am

DECEMBER

Date	Time	Sign	New Time
2	3:08 am	2 ♏	9:44 am
4	7:13 am	4 ♐	12:59 pm
6	4:46 pm	6 ♑	6:16 pm
8	8:07 pm	9 ♒	2:30 am
11	6:09 am	11 ♓	1:41 pm
13	7:35 pm	14 ♈	2:15 am
16	6:41 am	16 ♉	1:49 pm
18	4:37 pm	18 ♊	10:37 pm
21	3:13 am	21 ♋	4:22 am
23	2:25 am	23 ♌	7:51 am
25	4:28 am	25 ♍	10:14 am
27	7:21 am	27 ♎	12:38 pm
29	10:05 am	29 ♏	3:49 pm
31	2:57 pm	31 ♐	8:21 pm

Moon Void-of-Course Data for 2011

JANUARY

Last Aspect Date Time	New Sign Sign New Time
2 9:08 pm	3 ♑ 2:39 am
5 7:15 am	5 ♒ 11:08 am
7 3:51 pm	7 ♓ 9:57 pm
10 6:12 am	10 ♈ 10:24 am
12 9:47 pm	12 ♉ 10:37 pm
15 7:47 am	15 ♊ 8:23 am
17 12:57 pm	17 ♋ 2:29 pm
19 4:26 pm	19 ♌ 5:16 pm
21 1:57 pm	21 ♍ 6:10 pm
23 3:08 pm	23 ♎ 6:59 pm
25 5:04 pm	25 ♏ 9:15 pm
27 10:01 pm	28 ♐ 1:55 am
30 5:10 am	30 ♑ 9:04 am

FEBRUARY

Last Aspect Date Time	New Sign Sign New Time
1 2:32 pm	1 ♒ 6:21 pm
4 1:11 am	4 ♓ 5:24 am
6 2:13 pm	6 ♈ 5:45 pm
9 2:31 am	9 ♉ 6:22 am
11 2:27 pm	11 ♊ 5:20 pm
13 10:19 pm	14 ♋ 12:48 am
16 2:06 am	16 ♌ 4:14 am
18 3:36 am	18 ♍ 4:39 am
20 2:18 am	20 ♎ 4:01 am
22 3:35 am	22 ♏ 4:29 am
24 6:14 am	24 ♐ 7:46 am
26 1:08 pm	26 ♑ 2:32 pm
28 11:03 pm	3/1 ♒ 12:14 am

MARCH

Last Aspect Date Time	New Sign Sign New Time
2/28 11:03 pm	1 ♒ 12:14 am
3 9:36 am	3 ♓ 11:47 am
5 11:34 pm	6 ♈ 12:14 am
8 11:04 am	8 ♉ 12:52 pm
11 12:26 am	11 ♊ 12:31 am
13 9:10 am	13 ♋ 10:29 am
15 6:05 am	15 ♌ 3:33 pm
17 3:58 pm	17 ♍ 4:53 pm
19 2:10 pm	19 ♎ 4:03 pm
21 2:35 pm	21 ♏ 3:17 pm
23 4:08 pm	23 ♐ 4:45 pm
25 9:25 pm	25 ♑ 9:57 pm
27 11:17 pm	28 ♒ 7:00 am
30 6:21 pm	30 ♓ 6:38 pm
31 9:44 am	4/2 ♈ 7:16 am

APRIL

Last Aspect Date Time	New Sign Sign New Time
3/31 9:44 am	2 ♈ 7:16 am
4 6:04 am	4 ♉ 7:46 pm
5 7:02 pm	7 ♊ 7:22 am
8 10:24 pm	9 ♋ 5:02 pm
11 8:05 am	11 ♌ 11:37 pm
13 3:58 pm	14 ♍ 2:40 am
15 4:49 pm	16 ♎ 2:59 am
17 10:44 am	18 ♏ 2:19 am
20 12:53 am	20 ♐ 2:50 am
21 12:57 pm	22 ♑ 6:24 am
23 8:13 pm	24 ♒ 1:59 pm
26 7:28 am	27 ♓ 12:57 am
27 3:53 pm	29 ♈ 1:33 pm

MAY

Last Aspect Date Time	New Sign Sign New Time
1 11:20 am	2 ♉ 1:58 am
3 2:51 am	4 ♊ 1:09 pm
6 4:12 pm	6 ♋ 10:32 pm
9 2:52 am	9 ♌ 5:35 am
11 12:52 am	11 ♍ 9:59 am
12 10:52 pm	13 ♎ 11:56 pm
15 12:01 pm	15 ♏ 12:31 pm
17 7:09 am	17 ♐ 1:22 pm
19 10:17 am	19 ♑ 4:16 pm
21 5:04 pm	21 ♒ 10:32 pm
24 3:40 am	24 ♓ 8:24 am
25 2:15 pm	26 ♈ 8:36 pm
29 6:28 am	29 ♉ 9:02 am
31 11:37 am	31 ♊ 7:56 pm

JUNE

Last Aspect Date Time	New Sign Sign New Time
3 4:08 am	3 ♋ 4:36 am
5 1:33 am	5 ♌ 11:03 am
7 11:27 am	7 ♍ 3:33 pm
9 4:13 am	9 ♎ 6:31 pm
11 4:04 am	11 ♏ 8:33 pm
13 1:43 pm	13 ♐ 10:38 pm
15 11:31 pm	16 ♑ 1:59 am
18 4:07 am	18 ♒ 7:47 am
20 4:23 pm	20 ♓ 4:45 pm
21 10:51 pm	23 ♈ 4:24 am
24 6:07 pm	25 ♉ 4:53 pm
27 12:24 pm	28 ♊ 3:56 am
30 3:33 am	30 ♋ 12:13 pm

JULY

Last Aspect Date Time	New Sign Sign New Time
1 7:37 am	2 ♌ 5:43 pm
3 12:25 pm	4 ♍ 9:15 pm
5 8:19 pm	6 ♎ 11:54 pm
8 2:29 am	9 ♏ 2:31 am
10 9:05 am	11 ♐ 5:47 am
12 8:21 am	13 ♑ 10:14 am
15 2:40 am	15 ♒ 4:30 pm
17 8:23 am	18 ♓ 1:13 am
20 7:15 am	20 ♈ 12:25 pm
22 5:34 pm	23 ♉ 12:58 am
25 9:12 am	25 ♊ 12:34 pm
27 8:35 pm	27 ♋ 9:11 pm
28 7:03 pm	30 ♌ 2:16 am

AUGUST

Last Aspect Date Time	New Sign Sign New Time
1 2:20 pm	1 ♍ 4:41 am
1 7:38 am	3 ♎ 6:04 am
5 7:56 am	5 ♏ 7:57 am
7 11:14 am	7 ♐ 11:21 am
9 4:24 pm	9 ♑ 4:38 pm
10 4:34 pm	11 ♒ 11:47 pm
14 8:25 am	14 ♓ 8:54 am
15 4:21 am	16 ♈ 8:01 pm
19 7:50 am	19 ♉ 8:36 am
21 7:59 pm	21 ♊ 8:53 pm
24 5:33 am	24 ♋ 6:31 am
25 9:04 am	26 ♌ 12:09 pm
28 1:11 pm	28 ♍ 2:13 pm
29 6:15 pm	30 ♎ 2:25 pm

SEPTEMBER

Last Aspect Date Time	New Sign Sign New Time
1 1:35 pm	1 ♏ 2:48 pm
3 3:41 pm	3 ♐ 5:03 pm
5 8:30 pm	5 ♑ 10:03 pm
7 4:35 pm	8 ♒ 5:42 am
10 1:32 pm	10 ♓ 3:26 pm
12 9:45 pm	13 ♈ 2:49 am
15 1:10 pm	15 ♉ 3:25 pm
18 3:09 am	18 ♊ 4:06 am
20 12:33 pm	20 ♋ 2:53 pm
22 9:22 pm	22 ♌ 9:55 pm
24 10:39 pm	25 ♍ 12:49 am
25 3:47 pm	27 ♎ 12:51 am
28 9:51 pm	29 ♏ 12:05 am
30 10:17 pm	10/1 ♐ 12:42 am

OCTOBER

Last Aspect Date Time	New Sign Sign New Time
9/30 10:17 pm	1 ♐ 12:42 am
3 1:37 am	3 ♑ 4:16 am
5 1:58 am	5 ♒ 11:18 am
7 6:08 pm	7 ♓ 9:13 pm
8 12:51 pm	10 ♈ 8:57 am
12 8:08 pm	12 ♉ 9:35 pm
15 6:51 am	15 ♊ 10:15 am
17 6:18 pm	17 ♋ 9:38 pm
19 11:30 pm	20 ♌ 6:06 am
22 8:34 am	22 ♍ 10:40 am
23 4:47 pm	24 ♎ 11:49 am
26 8:18 am	26 ♏ 11:08 am
28 7:49 am	28 ♐ 10:45 am
30 9:30 am	30 ♑ 12:39 pm

NOVEMBER

Last Aspect Date Time	New Sign Sign New Time
1 5:00 pm	1 ♒ 6:08 pm
3 11:40 pm	4 ♓ 3:18 am
5 4:05 am	6 ♈ 2:02 pm
9 12:46 am	9 ♉ 2:45 am
11 11:27 am	11 ♊ 3:10 pm
13 10:42 pm	14 ♋ 2:19 am
16 12:22 am	16 ♌ 11:17 am
18 2:05 pm	18 ♍ 5:19 pm
20 5:21 pm	20 ♎ 8:16 pm
22 6:04 pm	22 ♏ 8:58 pm
24 6:04 pm	24 ♐ 8:57 pm
26 7:06 pm	26 ♑ 10:05 pm
28 6:01 pm	29 ♒ 2:02 am

DECEMBER

Last Aspect Date Time	New Sign Sign New Time
1 6:27 am	1 ♓ 9:45 am
2 1:06 pm	3 ♈ 8:51 pm
6 6:13 am	6 ♉ 9:34 am
8 6:39 pm	8 ♊ 9:52 pm
11 5:24 am	11 ♋ 8:26 am
13 11:05 am	13 ♌ 4:48 pm
15 8:20 pm	15 ♍ 10:58 pm
17 9:29 pm	18 ♎ 3:06 am
20 4:49 am	20 ♏ 5:33 am
22 4:49 am	22 ♐ 7:03 am
24 6:36 am	24 ♑ 8:47 am
26 8:36 am	26 ♒ 12:14 pm
28 4:31 pm	28 ♓ 6:45 pm
30 8:37 am	31 ♈ 4:48 am

Find the Magic in the Mundane

How can we stay grounded amid the hustle and bustle of today? Try working with the elements— earth, air, fire, and water—to reconnect with what's important in life.

From spiritual housecleaning to sex magic with your clothes on, beginners and longtime practitioners will find dozens of ways to magically enhance everyday life. This edition includes articles—grouped by element—on Pagan permaculture, fabric magic, foot magic, mantras, ornithomancy, fire dancing rituals, making a divining bowl, using the home as a magical tool, powerful effigies, tarot spell dowsing, and much more.

TELL US WHAT YOU THINK!

At Llewellyn our aim is to keep pace with your passion for lifelong learning and magical living. Please help us to understand and serve you better by taking our short survey (approx. 5 minutes).

Please go to
http://www.llewellyn.com/surveys.php
to complete the online questionnaire and let your voice be heard.
Thanks in advance for your feedback!

GET SOCIAL WITH **LLEWELLYN**

Find us on Facebook and Twitter

www.Facebook.com/LlewellynBooks
www.Twitter.com/Llewellynbooks

GET MORE AT **LLEWELLYN.COM**

Visit us online to browse hundreds of our books and decks, plus sign up to receive our e-newsletters and exclusive online offers.

- Free tarot readings • Spell-a-Day • Moon phases
- Recipes, spells, and tips • Blogs • Encyclopedia
- Author interviews, articles, and upcoming events

Notes:

Notes:

Notes:

Notes: